DEVELOPING YOUR THEORETICAL ORIENTATION IN COUNSELING AND PSYCHOTHERAPY

Third Edition

DUANE A. HALBUR
Georgia Military College
Life Management Group, Inc.

KIMBERLY VESS HALBUR
Medical College of Georgia at Georgia Regents University

PEARSON

Boston   Columbus   Indianapolis   New York   San Francisco   Hoboken
Amsterdam   Cape Town   Dubai   London   Madrid   Milan   Munich   Paris   Montréal   Toronto
Delhi   Mexico City   São Paulo   Sydney   Hong Kong   Seoul   Singapore   Taipei   Tokyo

Vice President and Editorial Director:
  Jeffery W. Johnston
Vice President and Publisher:
  Kevin M. Davis
Editorial Assistant: *Caitlin Griscom*
Executive Field Marketing Manager:
  Krista Clark
Senior Product Marketing Manager:
  Christopher Barry
Project Manager: *Lauren Carlson*
Procurement Specialist: *Pat Tonneman*
Senior Art Director: *Jayne Conte*
Cover Designer: *Nesbitt Graphics*
Cover Art: *Shutterstock/Det-anan*
Full-Service Project Management:
  Niraj Bhatt/Aptara®, Inc.
Composition: *Aptara®, Inc.*
Printer/Binder: *Courier-Westford*
Cover Printer: *Courier-Westford*
Text Font: *10 pt Janson Text LT Std*

Credits and acknowledgments for material borrowed from other sources and reproduced, with permission, in this textbook appear on the appropriate page within the text.

Every effort has been made to provide accurate and current Internet information in this book. However, the Internet and information posted on it are constantly changing, so it is inevitable that some of the Internet addresses listed in this textbook will change.

Copyright © 2015, 2011, 2006 by Pearson Education, Inc. All rights reserved. Manufactured in the United States of America. This publication is protected by Copyright, and permission should be obtained from the publisher prior to any prohibited reproduction, storage in a retrieval system, or transmission in any form or by any means, electronic, mechanical, photocopying, recording, or likewise. To obtain permission(s) to use material from this work, please submit a written request to Pearson Education, Inc., Permissions Department, 221 River Street, Hoboken, NJ 07030.

Library of Congress Cataloging-in-Publication Data

Halbur, Duane.
    Developing your theoretical orientation in counseling and psychotherapy/Duane A. Halbur, Kimberly Vess Halbur.—Third edition.
      pages cm
    Includes bibliographical references and index.
    ISBN 978-0-13-348893-7
    ISBN 0-13-348893-4
    1. Psychology—Philosophy.   2. Counseling.   3. Psychotherapy.   I. Halbur, Kimberly Vess.   II. Title.
    BF38.H33 2015
    158.3—dc23

2014011528

10 9 8 7 6 5 4 3 2 1

PEARSON

ISBN 10:   0-13-348893-4
ISBN 13: 978-0-13-348893-7

*In memory of
Edna May Thompson
and
Carol Lynn Halbur,
who gave us much love and many of our theories about life
and helped us to pass them along to our children
Dominic Anthony Halbur
and
Carolyn Maye Halbur*

About the Authors

Dr. Duane Halbur's research interests include the needs of school counselors, philosophical counseling, and the integration of technology in counseling. Along with teaching and writing, he works as a licensed counselor in private practice specializing in children and families in transition. Dr. Kimberly Vess Halbur's research includes cultural competencies for the helping professions and medical fields.

Preface

We first wrote *Developing Your Theoretical Orientation in Counseling and Psychotherapy* with the objective of assisting other helping professionals through finding their theoretical orientation more easily than we did. We realize that the term *helping professionals* may seem generic, but we use it in an effort to include helpers who work with diverse populations in a wide array of fields. Specifically, we are speaking to mental health counselors, psychologists, social workers, school counselors, substance abuse counselors, psychotherapists, and peer helpers. This third edition attempts to assist clinicians further in finding their theoretical orientation in a diverse society while enjoying the process of self-exploration. The theories are presented in a way that allows the reader to identify quickly the philosophical and cultural foundations of the theories while accessing the goals and techniques of the theories.

Because the work of helping professionals needs to be grounded in theory, we have featured in this text an innovative model for selecting a theoretical orientation and hands-on activities to assist readers in their quest for a theoretical approach to helping. Learning activities, reflection questions, and case studies are included throughout the text, with several featured prominently in Chapter 5. These activities have been updated to demonstrate traditional and contemporary theories as well as multicultural perspectives so important to the helping fields.

The Intentional Theory Selection (ITS) model is a contemporary model for selecting a theoretical orientation. This model can assist helpers in finding a theory that is congruent with their personal values. We also acknowledge that the selection of a theoretical orientation may be quite cyclical. Just as in life, change in theoretical orientation is constant and inevitable. Thus, a professional helper may revisit the model many times throughout his or her career.

This text may also serve as a reminder or overview of the foremost helping theories and their respective schools of thought. We provide readers with a reminder of the basic philosophies, goals, and techniques of the major theories of counseling. We hope this text offers just enough information to remind professional helpers of what they already know while enticing them to seek out and learn more about a presented theory.

In addition to a summary of selected counseling theories, students and counselors will be exposed to 10 applied ways to aid in the self-discovery process. This self-discovery will begin the readers' processes of intentionally finding a theoretical orientation that is congruent with their own worldview, beliefs, and values. The Selective Theory Sorter–Revised (STS–R) is a survey that was developed to help students and counselors discover which researched theories they might endorse. This sorter, more important in self-discovery than in assessment, is one of several tools that will be offered to readers while they are in the process of finding their own theoretical orientation.

We hope that readers find the material and the ITS model refreshing and at the same time meaningful. Those in the helping professions know, through research and observation, that theory is important. Many innovators, researchers, and clinicians have dedicated their research and life work to finding techniques and philosophies that can best serve our clientele. We owe so much to these pioneers who have helped us to be effective and ethical in the work we do.

The helping professions are truly important to a developing society. Helping professionals have the opportunity to prevent and remediate when they serve in a field that makes its daily impact by improving the lives of others. As you work on your own professional identity and struggles, remember that this opportunity is both a blessing and a responsibility. In this text, as in many endeavors in your professional life, you will be asked to look inward. As professionals, we ask this of clients; as authors, we ask this of you. Take this opportunity to challenge yourself and grow.

We have presented the ITS model and the STS–R at many professional conferences and have greatly appreciated the feedback and the anticipation for this project to be in print for a third time. We still receive emails and phone calls from faculty members who have adopted the text and their students who have enjoyed using it. The interest we have received professionally has served as a muse and motivation for us to improve and update it in this third edition.

NEW TO THIS EDITION

The third edition of *Developing Your Theoretical Orientation in Counseling and Psychotherapy* offers the following new elements:

- An increased focus on diversity, including commentary regarding the application of each theory in a culturally rich profession.
- A greater review of the implications of empirically validated treatments.
- A greater review of the implications of common-factor approaches to counseling.
- An expansion and update of the counseling theories, which are necessary for the successful completion of national and state counselor examinations, including updated techniques.
- Greater explanation of the application of multicultural counseling and feminism.
- Increased focus on material that readers will find relevant to Counseling for Accreditation of Counseling and Related Educational Programs™ (CACREP) 2016 Standards.
- Updated websites related to theories and theoretical training to allow readers quick access to more information.
- Updated cases to assist readers through the process of choosing their theoretical orientation.

With the addition of several new topics, the references have been updated significantly since the previous editions. Readers with experience with the first and second editions will also note a more consistent voice throughout the text.

We would like to thank the reviewers of our manuscript for their insights and comments: John P. Galassi, University of North Carolina at Chapel Hill; Terence Patterson, University of San Francisco; David Shriberg, Loyola University of Chicago; and Amy M. Williams, University of Northern Colorado.

Contents

CHAPTER ONE
Why Theoretical Orientation is Important   1

    A PERSONAL EXPERIENCE   1
    THE BIG PUZZLE   2
    WHAT IS THEORETICAL ORIENTATION?   3
    THE HELPER'S TOOL BELT   3
    WHAT CAN A THEORETICAL ORIENTATION DO FOR ME?   4
    HOW HAVE OTHERS PICKED A THEORETICAL ORIENTATION?   5
    WHAT IF I'M ECLECTIC?   6
    EMPIRICALLY VALIDATED THERAPIES: ARE THEY BETTER?   8
    GUIDANCE FROM COMMON FACTORS: DO THEY ALL WORK?   9
    ONCE I HAVE IT, HOW CAN I USE IT?   10
    HOW ARE THEORETICAL ORIENTATION AND ETHICS RELATED?   10
    THE MAIN POINTS   11
    REFLECTION QUESTIONS   11

CHAPTER TWO
Incorporating Theory into Practice   13

    MAKING THEORY USEFUL: A MODEL   13
    THEORY DEVELOPMENT   14
    IMPORTANCE OF YOUR LIFE PHILOSOPHY   15
    LIFE PHILOSOPHY—IT's PERSONAL   16
    SCHOOLS OF THOUGHT   17
    THEORIES   18
    GOALS AND TECHNIQUES: INTERVENTIONS AT WORK   19

COUNSELORS ARE DIVERSE   20

RESISTANCE TO THEORIES: ECLECTIC, INTEGRATED, OR JUST DON'T KNOW   21

DOES IT REALLY WORK?   23

WHAT TO TAKE HOME   24

REFLECTION QUESTIONS   25

CHAPTER THREE
Top 10 Ways to Find Your Theoretical Orientation   27

FIND YOURSELF   28

ARTICULATE YOUR VALUES   29

SURVEY YOUR PREFERENCES   30

USE YOUR PERSONALITY   30
   Taking the MBTI   37

CAPTURE YOURSELF   37

LET OTHERS INSPIRE YOU IN YOUR LEARNING   38

READ ORIGINAL WORKS   38

GET REAL   38

STUDY WITH A MASTER   39

BROADEN YOUR EXPERIENCES   40

TOP 10 WRAP-UP   40

REFLECTION QUESTIONS   41

SUGGESTED READINGS AND WEBPAGES   41

CHAPTER FOUR
Six Schools of Thought and Their Theories of Helping   45

PSYCHODYNAMIC SCHOOL OF THOUGHT   48
   Psychoanalytic Theory   48
   Analytical Theory   53
   Individual Psychology   55

BEHAVIORAL SCHOOL OF THOUGHT   58
   Behavioral Therapy   58

HUMANISTIC SCHOOL OF THOUGHT   61
   Person-Centered   62
   Existential   64
   Gestalt   67

PRAGMATIC SCHOOL OF THOUGHT   70
   Cognitive-Behavioral   70
   Rational Emotive Behavioral Therapy   72
   Reality Therapy   74

CONSTRUCTIVIST SCHOOL OF THOUGHT   76
   Multicultural Counseling and Therapy   77
   Feminist Therapy   79
   Narrative Therapy   81
   Solution-Focused Brief Therapy   84

FAMILY APPROACHES SCHOOL OF THOUGHT   86
   Bowen Family Systems Therapy   86
   Strategic Family Therapy   88
   Structural Family Therapy   89
   Family Therapies and Diversity   91

SUMMARY   92

REFLECTION QUESTIONS   92

CHAPTER FIVE
Case Examples for Integrating Theory into Practice   93

CLINICIAN CASE STUDIES   93
   Case One: Evan   93
   Case Two: Jill   95
   Case Three: Garrett   97
   Case Four: Lillian   99
   Comment on the Cases   101

CLIENT CASE STUDIES   102
   Case One: Tony   102
   Case Two: Nancy   102
   Case Three: Brenda   103

SUPERVISION CASE STUDIES 104
    Case One: Grace 104
    Case Two: Casey 104
    Case Three: Dominic 105
    Summary of Supervision Case Studies 106

PUTTING IT ALL TOGETHER 106
    Importance Revisited 106
    How Theory Is Found 106
    Benefit of the ITS Model to the Field 107

References 109

Index 115

Why Theoretical Orientation is Important

A PERSONAL EXPERIENCE

Since our first years of teaching graduate counseling classes, students have often asked, "How did you decide your theoretical orientation?" This question is reasonable and understandable because students in the helping professions are frequently asked about their theoretical orientation. Thus, we began pondering the development of our own theoretical orientations, which centered inevitably around three core issues: personalities, mentors and supervisors, and clients.

First, we contemplated how personality might play a role in the theories that we liked and the ways we worked with clients. For example, one of us is an outgoing, energetic person who reflects these traits in interactions with others, both personally and professionally, and who sets high standards and believes that, in general, people strive to do what they believe is right. The other tends to focus on philosophical understanding, however, and consequently practices existential questioning in everyday life. These personal tendencies greatly influence our theories. One of us focuses on social and humanistic theories, while the other works with theories that have strong philosophical foundations. Personal qualities, values, actions, and assumptions clearly have an impact on our theoretical orientations and consequently on our work with clients.

Next, we thought about our mentors and supervisors and the various theoretical orientations they espoused. For instance, one mentor was very clearly humanistic and relied on Gestalt interventions. Some faculty members were fairly diverse in their theoretical orientations and championed constructivist, client-centered, cognitive-behavioral, and ecological approaches. One clinical supervisor said that he was a "planned eclectic." These mentors and supervisors greatly affected our choices of theoretical orientation. Their feedback, guidance, and expectations were always tinted by their theoretical orientations. As a result, we knew that they had affected our choices as well; we were just not sure how.

Acknowledging that we had been exposed to a wealth of theoretical orientations, we began to think about past and present clients with whom we had worked. We thought about how effective our theoretical orientations were for them. We concluded that each client must have also affected us as we selected our theoretical orientations. Despite, or perhaps because of, our examinations of these theoretical orientation issues, we seemed to answer students by saying, "You just figure it out as you go along. When a theory really 'fits' for you, you will know it."

But we knew this answer was not satisfactory. We remembered all too well our first years as helping professionals. We had often been quizzed about our own theoretical orientations and yet we had not been given any tools other than the required survey course in major theories to guide us. As we recounted our own similar struggles, we were reminded in many ways just how important theoretical orientation is in the helping professions. Thus, we wanted to offer clinicians and our students specific strategies to use in developing their theoretical orientation.

THE BIG PUZZLE

Selecting a theoretical orientation is typically a puzzling experience for students in the helping professions. A common goal of training programs is to teach effective helping skills. Academic programs also strive to help students conduct counseling in a way that is intentional and theory based. Consequently, students are frequently asked during the course of their graduate programs to state their theoretical orientation, typically by writing a paper about it. The assignment usually goes something like this: After reading a brief overview of counseling theories, which one do you believe fits your style of counseling?

Although this assignment is valuable, it may occur too early in the education of professional helpers. Because these students do not yet have enough clinical experience to guide them, they typically respond to the theoretical orientation assignment by picking theories that sound good on paper. Students at this stage usually have little understanding of the theories they choose. Unfortunately, many students continue to support, research, and apply their chosen theory, which ultimately limits their overall understanding of counseling theories. Some students simply choose the instructor's theoretical orientation in hope of receiving a high grade on the assignment. Others pick the theory that they understand best. It is not that students are attempting to be lazy or manipulate instructors for a higher grade; rather, they are overwhelmed by the multitude of theories and therapeutic interventions to which they are exposed. Even when students find theories that they like on paper, they often feel lost and unable to apply theory to practice. Hence, most students in the helping professions find it extremely difficult to develop and articulate in both words and practice their own theoretical orientation. This dilemma can easily be compared to the experience of holding pieces to a jigsaw puzzle without having the picture on the front of the box that contained the puzzle pieces. In this situation, the corner and the edge pieces are easily identified, but the central pieces are difficult to discern.

On the journey to finding a theoretical orientation, the role of soul searching and clinical practice cannot be emphasized enough. Although this text does not offer direct clinical experience, it does provide for self-evaluation and soul searching. This text does offer applied methods to assist students and clinicians as they look for their theory of counseling. Within these pages you will first be offered the Intentional Theory Selection (ITS) model, which can serve as a guide to make finding your theoretical orientation a process. Tools, such as the Selective Theory Sorter–Revised (STS–R), will also be offered to serve as pragmatic assistants. Many resources, theory summaries, reflective questions, and case studies will also be offered to help clinicians and counselors-in-training begin to complete a puzzle that culminates in forming their theoretical orientation.

WHAT IS THEORETICAL ORIENTATION?

Before students in the helping professions can begin the voyage to finding and solidifying a theoretical orientation, they must have a working definition of the term *theoretical orientation*. This definition enables students, counselors, and the field in general to have a similar idea of what being theoretically orientated means. Poznanski and McLennan (1995) provide an excellent definition: A theoretical orientation is "a conceptual framework used by a counselor to understand client therapeutic needs" (p. 412). More specifically, theoretical orientation provides helpers with a theory-based framework for "(a) generating hypotheses about a client's experience and behavior, (b) formulating a rationale for specific treatment interventions, and (c) evaluating the ongoing therapeutic process" (Poznanski & McLennan, 1995, p. 412). Thus, theoretical orientation forms the foundation for helping professionals in counseling, social work, and applied psychology. Having a theoretical orientation provides helpers with goals and techniques that set the stage for translating theory into practice (Strupp, 1955).

As students in the helping professions learn skills and theories, they often struggle with ways to integrate the information. Yet theory and practical application need a balance (Drapela, 1990). In counseling classes, for example, students may learn to express empathy and to confront, but they do not yet understand how to practice those skills with the intention that follows from a specific theoretical orientation. By choosing a theoretical orientation to practice and applying it, a counselor is able to use general counseling skills in an applied and intentional way.

THE HELPER'S TOOL BELT

Once counselors learn the basic helping skills, they have the opportunity to use them in an intentional way. In many ways, a theoretical orientation serves as a tool belt. The tool belt is filled with a multitude of tools that serve different functions. Among the tools, counselors will find the basic skills of confrontation, reflection of feeling, open-ended questions, and empathy. Additionally, counselors who have a theoretical foundation have tools specific to their theory. For example, a Gestalt counselor has the tool of the *empty-chair technique,* and the behaviorist counselor has the tool of *behavioral contracting.* Any of these tools can be useful in the construction (helping) process. All of the techniques have the potential of achieving the same desired result: helping the client. The difficult part is knowing when to use each tool. Continuing with the tool belt analogy, there is an old adage that says something like this: "If you only have a hammer, everything looks like a nail."

For example, a student enrolled in a graduate counseling program is seeing a client at his practicum site. The client, a college freshman, is very frustrated with her mother and anxious about going home over the holiday break. The student believes that the client needs to express her feelings toward her mother. Depending on the counselor's theoretical orientation, the tool selected for the expression of the client's feelings may vary. If the counselor prefers rational emotive behavioral therapy (REBT), he may explore with the client her beliefs about going home for the holidays. If the counselor works from an existential framework, he might encourage the client to be authentic with her mother regarding her feelings of frustration. If the counselor ascribes to Gestalt theory, however, he may decide to use the empty-chair technique, prompting the client to express her feelings during the session. In this particular case, the counselor decides to use the empty-chair technique. The intervention looks somewhat awkward, and the counselor is clearly uncomfortable with the intervention and the processing of it with his client. After the session, the counselor says to his instructor, "Wasn't that awful? I can't believe it didn't work. I really thought the client would like it." Unfortunately, the counselor picked an intervention that really was not in his typical tool belt because his natural theory was REBT. He used an intervention, a tool that was not congruent with his theory. Although you can use a wrench to pound a nail, it will likely not feel right and may not be as effective.

WHAT CAN A THEORETICAL ORIENTATION DO FOR ME?

A theoretical orientation provides helpers with a framework for therapy that sets the foundation for intentional counseling. For the counselor, being intentional is a prerequisite to ethical and effective helping. Theory is an important factor in structuring therapy and directing interventions (Hansen & Freimuth, 1997). Consequently, intentional counseling requires counselors to rely on their theoretical orientation to guide therapy. Thus, when counselors get lost in the therapeutic process, theory can provide a road map. Theory is also a way for counselors to organize and listen to data and information given to them by clients. A number of theories provide specific steps to treatment planning; these steps may assist counselors in being intentional and consistent in their role as a therapist. Ideally, counselors' interventions stem from their theoretical orientation; however, human beings do not fit neatly into categories. Hackney (1992) has written eloquently about theory and process, stating that, like human nature, "client problems are typically multidimensional" (p. 2). The following is a clinical example.

Louis, a 23-year-old, Mexican-American male seeks therapy. During the initial interview, he states: "I am a loser. I have a college degree and can't get a job. I don't ask people out on dates because I know they'll see immediately that I'm a loser. When I do go out to meet people, women seem to avoid me." The therapist believes the client has a problem with self-esteem. While self-esteem is an important facet of the client's experience, it needs to be viewed from a larger perspective. The client's problem seems to encompass his thinking, feeling, behavior, and interactions with the world around him. A therapist who has a specific theoretical orientation will be able to view the client holistically, knowing that the theory will provide a road map for the therapy.

Espousing a theoretical orientation to helping has numerous benefits for both clinicians and the clients they serve. Specifically, a theoretical orientation provides ways to organize client information. An orientation can also help intentionality and consistency within the work of a professional helper. Although the helper should understand what a theoretical orientation is, why it is important, and what it can do for both the client and the counselor, this information provides little help to a counselor who must pick a theory from which to work. The ways in which others have picked a theory may help students understand where they can go to pick a working theory.

HOW HAVE OTHERS PICKED A THEORETICAL ORIENTATION?

Hackney (1992) noted that most helpers choose their theoretical orientation based on one of three considerations: (1) the theoretical orientation of the helper's training program, (2) the helper's life philosophy, and/or (3) the helper's professional experience as a client. Some helpers also consider the evidence supporting the various therapies or even look at the common characteristics of effective therapies. While helpers commonly use these traditional methods to find their theoretical orientation, each has inherent pitfalls. The shortcomings of each of these methods will be discussed in order to provide a rationale for a new model of choosing a theory that is presented in Chapter 2.

First, initial training programs may or may not expose students to every theoretical orientation. For example, if faculty members at the same institution support the same theoretical orientation, they limit their students' exposure to the myriad of available theories. Conversely, if students enroll in an academic program where every faculty member has a different theoretical orientation, the students may receive mixed messages about "effective" therapy. Another potential difficulty for students is underexposure to the *process* of developing a personal orientation because faculties choose not to discuss their own theoretical orientations in hopes of being unbiased in their teaching. Thus, a theoretical orientation to helping cannot be based solely on students' training programs.

Second, some counselors base their theoretical orientation on their own personality and philosophy of life. This approach can also present difficulties. For example, counselors who are predominantly optimistic and believe the best about people may choose a humanistic approach. Other counselors may believe that people's thoughts are the core of their problems and choose REBT as a way to help clients develop more rational thinking. Both beliefs ultimately influence how counselors perceive, interact with, and treat their clients, even if those clients have a personality and worldview much different from those of the counselors. Although theory provides a framework for working with most clients, counselors must remember that each client is unique. A counselor must remain both open to experience and flexible with clients.

The third way helpers determine their theoretical orientation is through clinical experience, even though helpers may realize that their theoretical orientation does not fit for all clients or clinical situations. For example, counselors who favor a humanistic orientation may have difficulty in career-counseling settings. While these counselors may be skilled at the reflection of feeling, genuineness, and rapport building that lay at the core of the humanistic approach, their clients who are seeking résumé reviews and job information may feel frustrated when they get a "listening ear" but not the results they expected, such as direct advice on finding an internship or tips on interviewing. In such cases, counselors need to adjust their theory to fit the needs of the client.

The fourth strategy employed by counselors to determine their theoretical orientation is choosing an evidence-based theory. While this is a sound decision-making strategy, it may be difficult for counselors to find an evidence-based theory that fits their personality, values, and/or client needs. Those who choose their theory in this way limit themselves to theories that lend themselves to empirical testing and validation. For example, therapies that focus on helping clients strive toward actualization and personality change may not be easy to validate and thus may be ignored in the process of choosing a theoretical orientation.

Counselors not only must maintain their fundamental beliefs and values regarding the helping relationship but also must adapt their interventions to help the client. In the example of the humanist in the career-counseling situation, he may choose to hold onto the belief that people are basically good and striving for actualization. However, in an attempt to meet the needs of the client, the humanistic career counselor may be open to a change of perception—one that acknowledges that formal career exploration can lead to greater actualization. In another example, while attempting to be grounded in theory, a cognitive-behavioral therapist utilized cognitive techniques that were not appropriate for her client because the client had low intellectual functioning. In attempting to stay completely in harmony with her theory, the therapist was not meeting her client's needs. Consequently, she had to adapt her style and take a more behavioral approach.

WHAT IF I'M ECLECTIC?

Most examples provided in the text thus far highlight a counselor with one specific theoretical orientation. However, many counselors do not believe that one size fits all and believe that they can best serve their clients by offering a variety of approaches to their clients. Thus, they believe there is better efficacy in applying different theories and techniques to different clients. In general, *eclecticism* has been found to be a practiced theoretical orientation (Norcross, 1997), with many offering it as their primary identified theory. However, some cautions about eclecticism should be noted. First, eclecticism requires extensive training and competency, which beginning counselors typically lack (Norcross, 2005). To truly be an effective, eclectic counselor, clinicians should be able to be intentional in their application of techniques. They should have a great understanding of what techniques to apply when specific symptoms present or specific client characteristics emerge. Often those that purport to be eclectic share that their goals include assessing their clients, identifying clients' needs, and providing those techniques or therapies that would be most beneficial to the clients. This, however, takes a great deal of skill and knowledge. It is truly a daunting task, during the complex interchange of a therapy session, to assess a client and pull from one's repertoire the "right" technique or the "right "therapy" that will meet a presenting client's needs. In addition, many who identify as eclectic have not completely identified and acknowledged the differences between technique and theory. Most who identify as eclectic refer to the eclectic component of their work as the action stage where interventions are offered to clients. Thus a potentially more accurate way to describe their work is by saying that they offer a variety of techniques or interventions.

Most eclectic counselors have an overarching theory that guides their work. Although this may not be true of all eclectic counselors, in practice, most counselors have a theoretical orientation they lean toward or even consider their primary orientation. "Switching" theoretical orientations to meet client needs does indeed seem to make sense. In the field of counseling, however, theoretical orientation offers a framework for how a clinician might view development, pathology, and the counseling relationship itself. Altering one's view, or application of, such constructs while in the middle of a therapeutic relationship would seem to be almost risky to the productivity of therapy and could even be confusing to clients. If a clinician is to choose eclectic as an approach, however, it would seem that he or she should have a vast understanding of the theories and therapies they hope to utilize with clients. Thus, the authors of this text and many others recommend that beginning counselors may be best served by developing a single theoretical orientation that works best for them and learning to be as effective as possible within that paradigm.

However, eclecticism is indeed endorsed by many counselors, so its merit should not be just thrown out. Sometimes eclecticism is titled *strategic eclecticism*, highlighting the intentionality and purposefulness of using a wide variety of therapies and techniques. However, the authors offer a reframe. There is a difference between *being eclectic* and *applying a variety of techniques*. A counselor who is truly eclectic in terms of theory would change fundamental beliefs about human development, psychopathology, and epistemology from situation to situation and from client to client. However, applying a variety of techniques while maintaining a firm foundation in a fundamental belief is a different process. For example, an existential therapist working with a client with a phobia may use systematic desensitization (an eclectic technique for a traditional existentialist) while maintaining that removing such a phobia will enable the client to move toward greater actualization and live a more meaningful life (theoretically founded).

Being grounded in a theoretical orientation does not stop you from being flexible to the needs of clients. To truly serve clients, we should be fluid in the process and adaptable in the relationship. We should be willing, and competent, to be able to understand clients from a variety of perspectives. Their symptoms, characteristics, and immediate needs should affect how therapists work with clients. As a therapist works with diverse clients and their needs, however, flexibility and eclecticism in fundamental beliefs seems like a potential disservice not only to clients but also to therapists who strive to be congruent, ethical, and effective.

EMPIRICALLY VALIDATED THERAPIES: ARE THEY BETTER?

Similar to those who choose eclecticism as an answer to the question of theoretical orientation are those who choose how to work with clients based on research. Some clinicians and researchers believe that the best way to decide how to work with clients is by examining the research and seeing what, through scientific inquiry, we know are effective therapies. Research in the fields of counseling, psychology, and the related helping professions has produced a variety of *empirically validated therapies (EVTs)*, with a large number of those being "proven" (see Chamless et al., 1998) to work.

Those who promote using EVTs or *empirically supported treatments (ESTs;* see Parson, 2009) as the focus of their work worry less about what theory to "choose" and instead ask what technique or theory is "proven" to work with the client issue that is presented. To discover EVTs, specific techniques are typically applied to clients with an isolated or limited symptomology through the use of controlled research methods to see which therapies indeed prove to be most effective for specific clients and specific symptoms. This commonsense approach is becoming vastly popular through the helping professions; however, it does present some difficulties.

Many of these proven approaches specifically look at therapies that attempt to address one specific symptom. Most of the EVTs discovered do not promote client health and welfare or alleviate diagnosed disorders. They look instead at how specific symptoms can be reduced or eliminated. Thus, EVT techniques are predominately behavior-based because there is a propensity to measure symptoms while using these techniques.

Consequently, although the EVT argument is often presented as relevant when discussing clinicians choosing a theoretical orientation, most EVTs are not theories at all. This is partly because, for a therapy to be empirically validated, it must "be studied as a treatment for a disorder or problem, be manualized, and be validated either by two different studies done using a randomized clinical trials design, or by use of a single-subject design (traditionally of relevance primarily to behavioral therapies)" (Bohart, O'Hara, & Leitner, 1998, p. 142). Thus, they may be categorized more accurately as techniques or collections of interventions. In addition, many of these therapies do not, as a theory would, provide conceptualization of clients, perspectives of development, or frameworks for the progression of therapy. They are focused on the relief of specific symptoms and include approaches such as *interactive behavioral therapy (IBT)* for people with intellectual disabilities (Tomasulo & Razza, 2009), *dialectical behavioral therapy (DBT)* for people with borderline personality disorder (Hoffman & Steiner-Grossman, 2012) and for eating disorders (Safer, Telch, Chen, & Linhan, 2009), and *cognitive behavioral therapy* for panic disorder (Craske & Zunker, 2001).

Many of the studies validating these approaches analyze interventions and approaches with clients that have specific symptoms (Yalom, 2002) and not with clients with complicated diagnoses. Although there is scientific support for the use of empirically validated therapies, there is limited ability about generalizing findings to a diversity of clients and symptomologies. As Yalom (2002) states, however, "nonvalidated therapies are not invalidated therapies" (p. 223).

GUIDANCE FROM COMMON FACTORS: DO THEY ALL WORK?

Theories vary greatly in their depth, complexity, and usefulness. In the counseling field, there really could be as many theories, and there likely are, as there are counselors. However, the theoretical approaches that are generally published are those proven to have some generalized effectiveness (Kottler, 1999). Some answer the question of choosing their theoretical orientation by looking at the characteristics from all theories of counseling and examining the commonalities and the effectiveness about all of them. This so-called *dodo bird effect* states that factors common to all the various counseling theories account for the efficacy of all of the currently practiced psychotherapy theories (Leibert, 2011; Wampold, 2001). This effect states that we can find common, curative characteristics (Grencavage & Norcross, 1990) that occur in counseling and therapeutic relationships to explain why therapy ultimately works.

Wampold sought data for differential efficacies among therapies but discovered the opposite. Wampold ascribed this to the common factors theory of uniform efficacy among all existing psychotherapies. The idea that common factors among the different counselors are what account for their efficacy was first proposed by Rosenzweig (1936). This concept received little attention until nearly 40 years later, when Luborsky, Singer, and Luborsky (1975) found empirical data to suggest that all therapies had nearly equal outcomes, thereby confirming the accuracy of the dodo bird effect. Since that time, numerous studies have been done and articles have been written that support the dodo bird effect (Assay & Lambert, 1999; Duncan, 2002; Wampold et al., 1997).

Assay and Lambert (1999) concluded from their empirical study comparing various therapies that specific factors or techniques accounted for only 15% of the variance in treatment outcome, whereas common factors accounted for the remaining 85%. Specifically, they found that client factors (what the client brings to therapy) accounted for the majority of the variance in outcome (40%), followed by relationship factors (30%) and by placebo, hope, and expectancy (15%). Wampold (2001) offered similar common factors, including alliance, allegiance, adherence, and counselor effects.

Of particular importance are Assay and Lambert's (1999) expectancy factor and Wampold's (2001) allegiance factor. Expectancy involves the clients' belief in the credibility of the theory and thus their *expectation* that it will be helpful and produce positive change. Allegiance involves a condition similar to that of expectancy, except it is the counselor who must believe that the treatment he or she is offering is efficacious. The concepts of expectancy and allegiance parallel Frank's (1973) assertion that counseling is most helpful when both the client and the counselor believe in its efficacy. Arthur (2001) expressed a similar sentiment regarding efficacy in his review of studies on factors contributing to counselors' choices of theoretical orientation. These common factors lead to the first consideration for counselors-in-training when choosing a theoretical orientation: They must assess whether they believe in the theory themselves and whether they believe they can convey that conviction to clients sufficiently to gain their acceptance of the theory as well.

Finding what is common and effective in various theories of therapy has proven successful to researchers (eg., Grencavage & Norcross, 1990) and beneficial to clinicians (Halbur & Halbur, 2006) across the various counseling theories. If people accept wholeheartedly the premise of the dodo bird, then *what* theoretical orientation one chooses is not nearly as important as *that* a theoretical orientation is chosen. As stated above, research on common factors theory has suggested that, although all major theories have the potential for equally effective outcomes, counselors' belief in their theory is critical to its actual effectiveness (Arthur, 2001; Assay & Lambert, 1999; Frank, 1973; Wampold, 2001).

ONCE I HAVE IT, HOW CAN I USE IT?

Once a counselor's theoretical orientation is developed, it must be put into action. Counselors are often ready to jump in with one of the many techniques shown to be effective with clients (e.g., Erford, Eaves, Bryant, & Young, 2010). It is important to know first, however, how to move forward. Theoretical orientation is used as a blueprint to organize a client's information as well as a tool to guide clinical decisions, diagnosis, intervention selection, and treatment planning. Theoretical orientation can help determine the direction of and activities used during the course of counseling. Certainly, counselors use theory to explain or conceptualize clients' problems. According to Kottler (1999), theory is "the place to start when you are trying to sort out a complex, confusing situation" (p. 30). Similarly, Strohmer, Shivy, and Chodo (1990) suggest that counselors may also use theoretical orientation to confirm selectively their hypotheses regarding their clients. Not only does theoretical orientation help in case conceptualization, diagnosis, and treatment planning, but it may also allow for a clinician to behave ethically.

HOW ARE THEORETICAL ORIENTATION AND ETHICS RELATED?

Clinicians are ethically and often legally bound to have a theoretical foundation. Informed consent is a component of many professional ethical codes, including those of the American Counseling Association (ACA), the American Psychological Association (APA), and the National Association of Social Workers (NASW). Each of these professional ethics codes states that clients enter the helping relationship with informed consent. Implicit within the notion of informed consent is that helpers should share their theoretical orientation with clients or must at least be able to articulate their theory if asked by clients. Helpers who share their theoretical orientation with clients allow them to make an informed choice to engage in therapy. Thus, helpers need to be able to articulate their theoretical orientation and how it affects the helping relationship and the therapeutic process. In addition, many states dictate that licensed practitioners provide their clients with a professional disclosure statement. Such a statement usually orients the client to the counseling process and typically includes information about the helper's educational background and areas of expertise, the length of sessions, the responsibilities of each party, the hourly fee, and the helper's theoretical orientation. Thus, helpers need to be able to articulate their theoretical orientation in order to meet these ethical and professional obligations.

THE MAIN POINTS

In summary, counselors must develop a theoretical orientation that gives them the tools to build ethical, helping relationships based on their values, personality, and intention. Choosing a theory, "a conceptual framework used by a counselor to understand client therapeutic needs" (Poznanski & McLennan, 1995, p. 412), is an ongoing process that will ultimately make counselors more confident and effective in serving the needs of their clients. Within the chapter, the processes that counselors often engage in to determine their theory range from finding their theory based on their own therapeutic experiences to examining research on empirically validated therapies.

In the following chapters, readers will be assisted in developing their theoretical orientation through many forms of self-examination. The Intentional Theory Selection (ITS) model, which is presented in Chapter 2, offers a framework for finding a theoretical orientation. Chapter 3 builds on this model by offering reflection questions, activities, value clarification, and the Selective Theory Sorter as ways to help counselors understand theories that are most likely congruent with who they are and the potential work they do and will do with clients. In the remaining chapters, theory is offered in a pragmatic way following the ITS model, and clinical and supervisory examples of the ITS model in action are discussed.

REFLECTION QUESTIONS

1. If you had to select your theoretical orientation today, what would it be? How confident are you with your current choice of theoretical orientation?
2. What experiences have you had with clients that either support or negate your current theoretical orientation?
3. What influences have faculty members and supervisors had on your theoretical orientation?
4. What do you see as advantages and disadvantages to using empirically validated therapies?
5. What steps do you need to take to increase your allegiance to the theories in which you are interested?

Incorporating Theory into Practice

2

Practitioners and researchers alike contend that, for effective and intentional counseling to occur, helping professionals must adopt a comprehensive counseling theory. Theory serves as a conceptual framework and guide to interventions and assists helpers in the process of effective counseling. Thus, being theory driven is important, but clinicians have many theories to understand. And knowing the various theories and espousing one specific paradigm are not sufficient for helpers to translate theory into practice. Placing theory on a practical level requires more than textbook knowledge and a desire to be theory based. First, a helper must make an intentional cognitive shift. This shift, which is necessary for the most effective counseling, starts with a process of self-exploration; is built on a foundation of knowledge; and, if successful, culminates with the ability to move to client-counselor action. For the greatest therapeutic gains, helpers should begin to think in new ways. However, understanding and integrating a personal theory of counseling is often a foreign process, especially to the neophyte helper.

MAKING THEORY USEFUL: A MODEL

Making theory practical requires a process that starts with increased self-knowledge and ends with techniques to help clients. In counseling practicum and fieldwork courses, students often ask, "Now what do I do with him?" or "What technique do you think would be best to use with her now?" Although quite relevant, these questions are similar to a golfer asking a caddy which clubs to use before learning the art of the golf swing. For you, as a helper, to do ethical and intentional counseling, a process of development must occur.

This development is not a linear process. Cognitive and personal changes will likely occur as you have new experiences and learn more about yourself and the world around you. Consequently, beginning helpers, as well as the most seasoned professionals, will have moments where their theoretical orientation is challenged or influenced. Although challenges are difficult, the helper must undergo intentional development to become more confident and effective.

If traveled successfully, the road to development begins with self-reflection and ends with application. Making theory practical starts with the understanding of what we call *life philosophy*. Obviously, as your life experiences change, your view of the world also changes. Thus, your counseling theory and ultimately the techniques you use may change over the course of your career. A commonly expressed fear of many beginning counselors is that, once they have adopted one theory, it will be tattooed on their foreheads for all instructors, supervisors, and future clients to judge. This worry is unnecessary because, as helpers change, so may their theory.

THEORY DEVELOPMENT

Through self-awareness, helpers may begin the ongoing and ever-evolving process of theory development. This development will continue to unfold for helping professionals as their life philosophy changes through experiences and insight. Once a counselor has taken the first step of acquiring self-knowledge through experience, classes, and reading, the next step is to gain a general understanding of the six major schools of thought. The schools of thought serve almost as families of ideas, each with related yet unique members. About 250 established counseling theories have been identified, and these can typically be placed into families or schools of thought. These theories are often categorized together by identifying specific ideological similarities. One way to categorize theories is through the following six schools of thought: (1) *psychodynamic*, (2) *behavioral*, (3) *humanistic*, (4) *pragmatic*, (5) *constructivist*, and (6) *family approaches*. These schools of thought hold unique philosophies regarding human nature; thus, a general understanding of them is a key component in selecting a working theory. Each of these schools is represented by more specific, finely honed theories. For example, within the pragmatic school, several paramount theories exist, such as rational emotive behavioral therapy (REBT), which focuses on being rational and thinking logically. The related, yet contrasting, reality therapy focuses on taking control of one's actions and confronting the consequences (Corey, 2012). Adopting a specific theory from a school of thought is similar to picking a blue crayon from a package of 100 crayons that has several shades and hues of blue. Hence, like the color blue, the various theories in each school have hues that are similar yet distinct.

Once clinicians examine their life philosophy, adopt a school of thought, and select a specific theory, they are ready to take some action. At this stage, helping professionals need to develop goals and techniques for therapy that are supported by their theoretical orientation. This, too, is challenging because the uniqueness of clients frequently requires helping professionals to use different techniques, like pulling tools from a tool belt. Knowing which tool to access, however, requires having a working framework that is best supported by a strong foundation in theory.

Although the process of making theory practical may seem overwhelming now, it is manageable if helpers follow several steps, which are described in the next several

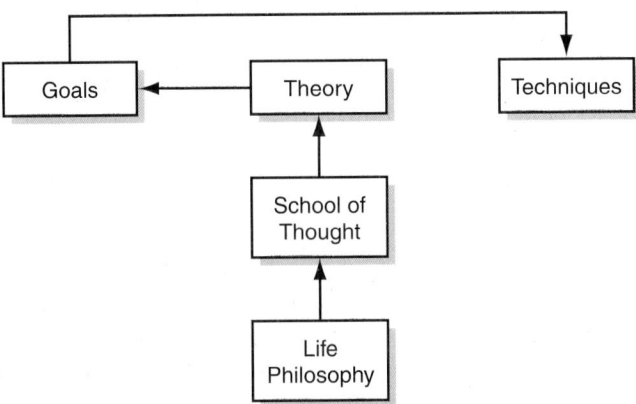

FIGURE 2.1 Intentional Theory Selection Model

sections. Later in the text, information, case studies, and activities are presented to help counselors gain awareness and make effective choices as they choose and solidify a theoretical orientation.

The Intentional Theory Selection (ITS) model of selecting a theoretical orientation is utilized as an example throughout this text (see Figure 2.1). The ITS model incorporates those aspects of theory selection that were found through research with students and counselors to be most significant in their personal solidification of theory. This model may be used to help counselors find not only their theoretical point of reference but also an orientation that is congruent with their individual values.

IMPORTANCE OF YOUR LIFE PHILOSOPHY

Life philosophy is the foundation of the ITS model. As a helper, being anchored in theory first requires that you have self-understanding and insight. You must become aware of how you view your world and must gain a greater comprehension of your own values (Hansen & Freimuth, 1997; Watts, 1993). Consider these questions: What is truth? Are people good? How do we gain knowledge? What causes behavior? Is spirituality important? What is right? It appears a revisit to Philosophy 101 is approaching. As a helper, however, you do not need to seek the writings of philosophers; instead, you have the opportunity to be introspective. You have the opportunity to look inside yourself and identify your own "assumptive world" (Hansen & Freimuth, 1997, p. 656). Your assumptive world is like a camera lens containing your ideas, beliefs, culture, and values; through this camera lens you perceive the world around you. Understanding how you view yourself, others, and the world around you is the first step in placing theory into a practical realm. These personal and motivating beliefs are core to your every action. Your schema of the world is not just essential to what you do but also ultimately the center of who you are. Helping professionals learn to help clients identify what they value and ultimately what gives meaning to their lives. As helpers incorporate theory into practice, they undergo a similar process. Once aware of your own views, you can move to adopting a counseling theory that not only serves clients in intentional ways but also complements who you are as a unique individual. An often-quoted phrase of Socrates, "The unexamined life is not worth living," holds true for helping professionals as well. Without understanding your own life philosophy, you will find it difficult to provide effective counseling.

An additional building block of life philosophy is what you find personally meaningful. Whether this belief comes from family, ethnicity, traditions, spirituality, or culture or is created personally, it will greatly affect how you work with clients. At the root of these questions—What keeps you going? What gives you inspiration? Why do you wake each day?—is an important revelation: your purpose, your life's meaning.

Your beliefs, values, and meanings are key components to who you are and your own subjective world. Yet you are so much more. As a multicultural individual, you are also a product of your culture, ethnicity, gender, family, sexual orientation, socioeconomic background, and religion. Your values and beliefs are founded on where you come from and where you intend to go. These differences may at times greatly affect your work as a counselor. For example, we once asked a class of ours, "What do you value?" We received the typical and expected answers—family, work, children, friends, being honest, working hard. However, several students had immediate, overt, nonverbal reactions when one international student responded, "Dependence." We asked these students to clarify their reactions, and they discussed their values of autonomy, empowerment, and independence. Their values, like their classmate's values, were greatly influenced by their cultural background and where they came from. You are influenced by your traditions and your adoption or adaptation of those traditions. Your life philosophy is indeed your own, yet it is made up of many influences.

Those working in the helping professions are becoming vastly more diverse, as are the clients served. As we pointed out to our class, values, beliefs, and worldviews are neither right nor wrong. It is paramount for helping professionals to identify their philosophy of life but not necessarily judge it. For example, is the student who valued dependence wrong? No. However, that student must understand her value and how it may affect her theoretical orientation and her work with clients. Conversely, those students who valued independence must understand that everyone does not hold this value. They must be careful about the assumptions they make about the personal worldviews of the clients they serve.

LIFE PHILOSOPHY—IT's PERSONAL

Identifying your life philosophy is likely the greatest challenge in finding your theoretical orientation. The most important questions are often the hardest. Many beginning counseling theories courses offer a culminating exercise that asks the developing clinicians to state their theoretical orientation of choice. This capstone project reflects the field's emphasis on theory and theoretical orientation. However, this creates strain and stress in some students. This occurs for many reasons; however, one paramount reason is that stating your theory, a reflection of your life philosophy, is actually a rather personal acknowledgment. Our theoretical orientation actually serves as a reflection of us—the values and beliefs that we hold dear. Sharing such personal information about ourselves places us in perceived vulnerable positions. We may feel vulnerable because there are only a few situations comparable to being questioned about our theoretical orientation. The first is in graduate training—often in a beginning course—a time where we already feel judged. The second is when we interview for positions as clinicians or educators. In this case, we also worry that our proclamation of a certain theory may either gain us acceptance or cause us rejection. Third, we are sometimes questioned about our theory by our clients. Typically clients are not asking us our theory to scrutinize it but to be informed and to understand what it is we might "do" to them.

It is important to remember that when we share our theory, it is the theoretical orientation of choice stemming from where we are in this particular point in life. One's life philosophy is an ever-changing, ever-emerging construct. Life events—those that are positive, those that are negative, and everything in between—affect, influence, and mold us. Just as the experiences therapists see their clients grapple with life-altering events, counselors, too, have life-changing experiences. Some of these are subtle—minor changes in financial status, schedule changes, or new information gained at a workshop. However, some of these may have far greater impacts. Family changes, major health changes, epiphanies in faith, career changes, the death of a partner, or having children are "everyday" events that change how one construes meaning about the surrounding world. Some of these experiences, even those that are happenstance, create an opportunity for clinicians to change. In times where meaningful experiences occur, therapists are not only likely to change their life philosophies but, perhaps, *should* change their life philosophies. It makes sense that therapists should allow life to happen and affect them, one hopes in positive ways. As change occurs, however, and worldviews remain fluid, counselors will change, too. Consequently, life philosophy, the foundation of the Intentional Theory Selection Model, will also change. Ultimately this means that, as counselors experience life, the work they do with their clients will alter. It is important, as a component of self-reflection and ethical practice, that counselors remain astute and aware of how their clients are affected by counselor changes.

SCHOOLS OF THOUGHT

The truly difficult step in adopting a theory for a counselor is gaining self-knowledge. Once you identify your own life philosophy, you can begin to examine the schools of thought that drive theory. This initial examination of theory requires only the willingness to read, listen, and comprehend. The information is available in this text and in a multitude of other resources. Beyond classroom lectures, you can find a bounty of literature describing the six schools of thought and their various theories (see Suggested Readings and Webpages at the end of Chapter 3). This step in the process toward adopting a theory is simple to learn. Knowing the multitude of facts surrounding each theorist, the counseling history, and the specific rhetoric of each school is not a prerequisite at this stage. However, you must begin to learn the basic assumptions of each theory, which will empower you to identify those theories that seem to hold assumptions similar to your own life philosophy. Consequently, you may take on a process of discovery in which you look for those applications that are congruent with the core of who you are.

Professional helpers are not in complete agreement on how many general schools of thought exist. However, they typically count four to six (e.g., Corsini, 1979; Halbur & Halbur, 2006; Halbur & Halbur, 2011; Ivey et al., 1997) families, schools, or clusters that have similarities among the theories within. We have identified six schools of thought: (1) psychodynamic, (2) behavioral, (3) humanistic, (4) pragmatic, (5) constructivist, and (6) family approaches. We debated how best to include family approaches and chose to consider them as a separate and unique school of thought. Many, and perhaps most, counselors do indeed acknowledge the use of family paradigms in their work with families and individuals. Consequently, it is likely that some narrative therapists (from the constructivist school of thought) would also acknowledge family systems (a major approach within the family approaches) as a vital part of their theoretical orientation. However, many clinicians work predominantly out of a family approach serving individuals, couples, and families, so including family approaches as an independent school is practical.

Although these schools of thought may seem distinct, similarities between them make the job of choosing one more challenging. However, these schools of thought are diverse in their assumptions regarding how personality develops, how pathology is perceived, how health is achieved, and what the role of the counselor is. For example, the counseling theory of existentialism within the humanistic school of thought espouses the idea that clients' health is achieved through helping them embrace meaning in their lives, while cognitive-behavioral approaches assist clients in developing more effective views of themselves and the world. While both approaches have proven successful in helping clients achieve more fulfilling lives, the underlying philosophies are quite different. Thus, helpers must first be oriented to the basic philosophies of the major schools of thought (see Chapter 4). Choosing your school of thought is ultimately an attempt to find a fit for you. Some schools of thought may leave you feeling that something is missing, while other schools may leave you feeling that you have found a natural match. However, choosing a school of thought will seem easier after you have completed the first step of personal reflection: looking at your life philosophy.

THEORIES

Once you have identified your life philosophy and have a general understanding of the school of thought that best fits your beliefs, you are ready to pick your theory or theories. This process begins when you gain a general understanding of the various theorists within the school of thought that is most congruent to your life philosophy (Watts, 1993). For example, within the psychodynamic school, do you agree with Sigmund Freud, who viewed humans as mostly sexual creatures, or with Alfred Adler, who saw humans primarily as social creatures? At this stage, you will likely begin looking for those theories that most parallel your own views by using a process of comparing and contrasting. As you pick the theory that matches your own most closely, you will begin to feel yourself gaining a stronger foundation.

In choosing your theory, you should understand that anyone can build a theory. However, the theoretical approaches that are generally published are those proven to have some generalized effectiveness (Kottler, 1999). As you move toward acceptance of a theory, you may experience times of anxiety or frustration in the process. You may sometimes find dissonance between your own beliefs and the theories with which you are confronted. This dissonance results in emotional consequences, which is part of a natural developmental process. Once you identify with a specific theory, however, you are likely to have a general sense of relief because you will find direction and may feel more confident in your interactions with clients (Mahoney, 1991). For example, one of our graduate students took the Selective Theory Sorter–Revised (STS–R) (in Chapter 3) and scored high on rational emotive behavioral therapy and the constructivist school of thought. She then took the advice later stated in Chapter 3 to learn more about those theories that she scored high on. She visited a webpage that streamed a video about Albert Ellis, the founder of REBT, that showed REBT in action. She found herself feeling dissonance because she did not like the persona she found in Ellis. Later, however, after she wrestled with her decision, she found the theory to be congruent with her and her reactions were really more in reaction to Ellis. She felt relief as she settled into her theory and is a practicing REBT therapist today.

Finding your theoretical orientation can be likened to a tree, with theory serving as the branches. Your life philosophy serves as your soil and nutrients, sustaining your actions. Your adopted school of thought is the trunk, holding all that you do with your clients. The branches, the theories you choose, support all that you demonstrate to clients and all that you do to serve them therapeutically. Finally, these theories determine what you actually give to your clients. The leaves and fruits, your goals and techniques, provide your clients supporting shade and give them sustenance to grow. Although this may seem ambiguous right now, as you read on, you will likely gain a better understanding of the schools of thought and their theories and how this will prepare you to provide counseling and psychotherapy that is intentional (see Chapter 4).

GOALS AND TECHNIQUES: INTERVENTIONS AT WORK

After making a theoretical choice, the next step for the helper is to adopt goals and techniques. Helpers should think ahead to the activities and interventions that will form their techniques (Jongsma & Peterson, 1995), which they will utilize when they provide counseling and therapy. What techniques you as a helper ultimately choose, however, will, and should, be based on your theoretical orientation, which will make you accountable for the therapeutic work you do with clients.

As a beginning counselor, you may decide or feel pressured to skip self-understanding and theoretical development and jump straight to applying goals and techniques. You rightfully want to know what to do, and you may believe that you should learn immediately how to help. In many training programs, however, discussing counseling techniques comes too early. In most programs, helpers often learn *how* to act as counselors before they learn *who* they are as counselors. This approach is often driven by the belief that counselors' training rests primarily on helping counselors know *what to do*. As a result of the widely accepted belief that the counselor is the true *instrument of change*, we run the risk of forgetting that counseling is ultimately a unique yet specified relationship. At a fundamental level, almost anyone can learn techniques. For example, the *empty-chair technique* requires that you ask clients to talk to someone as though that person were present when she is not (the empty chair). This technique is utilized to help individuals through various therapeutic challenges. Using this technique requires very simple instructions that a nonprofessional can understand. However, the ways in which you as a helper follow up on this intervention and respond to the client are based in your theory. Consequently, you should be theory based before you can be properly technique driven.

The argument for eclectic work is typically the strongest when it comes to choosing techniques. It is very common for counselors to be hesitant about limiting the number of techniques they use. This is an especially strong argument because some techniques do truly work better with some clients. As discussed in Chapter 1, we believe there is truly a difference between intentionally utilizing diverse techniques and being eclectic. If a technique from an alternate theory can help the counselor and client move forward in the change process, and if the technique is congruent with the therapeutic goals, it is ethical and valuable to be flexible in the therapy process. A narrative therapist, for example, would traditionally not utilize behavioral contracting. However, if a behavioral technique would help the client work toward goals that are congruent with narrative work, the counselor-client relationship remains founded on theoretical orientation.

As the counselor, you are the one who ultimately provides interventions that help your clients achieve their goals. Each theory and school of thought provides you with techniques and therapeutic goals that are appropriate, given *your* values and *your* clients' needs. If you have adopted a theoretical approach successfully, your effectiveness as a helper then depends on your ability to recognize with your clients their needs and to execute techniques congruent with your theory (e.g., Hansen, Rossberg, & Cramer, 1993). At this point, researchers and clinicians who have come before you have already done the work and the research, and you simply have to consult their teachings and writings. In this endeavor, you will learn quickly that the various schools, theories, and interventions strive to meet the needs and characteristics of a diverse society.

COUNSELORS ARE DIVERSE

Multicultural issues have been widely incorporated into counseling and its theoretical approaches. Integrating this facet of competence into your counseling approach first requires an understanding of the term *culture*. Culture is ultimately the rules, values, symbols, and ideologies of an identified group of people (Srebalus & Brown, 2001).

This general definition of culture should help you to see that an interactive society includes both separate and unique cultures. To understand the implications of culture, you must first understand your own culture and have a general understanding of other cultures with which you work. Diversity that comes from age, gender, race, socioeconomic class, ability, religion, and sexual orientation has a major impact on how relationships in general, as well as counselor-client relationships, develop and mature. Typically, the literature focuses on how counselors may work most effectively with clients who represent a population that is different from their own. Most of the literature assumes, however, that the counselor is of the dominant culture, and counselors see themselves more and more often represent underrepresented cultures.

For example, many counseling textbooks offer practical suggestions for working with clients who are gay, lesbian, bisexual, or transgender. Their authors stress that helpers must be in touch with their values and biases and that it is vital for them to consider the social environment pertinent to their clients. Issues specific to these populations, such as oppression and the coming-out process, are discussed, and primers on various cultures are offered. However, little practical support exists for the counselor who is from an underrepresented population. The question, How can a counselor work with a client *who is a lesbian*? is not unique and is addressed in the professional literature. However, the question, How can a counselor *who is a lesbian* work with clients? is often ignored. In this emerging field, helpers continue to build on the research and literature addressing the multicultural needs of their clients. However, counselors often struggle in addressing their own multicultural needs, backgrounds, and experiences.

Like clients, counselors also come from a variety of cultures and backgrounds. Their life philosophy and values, which are a dramatic component of their counseling approach, do influence how they interact with clients and direct what they believe is important for their clients. The ITS model utilized throughout this text offers great benefits to counselors across cultures of race, gender, sexual orientation, ability, religion, and age. As we have outlined, the foundation of this model begins with the identification of one's life philosophy. However, life philosophy is so deeply rooted in one's specific culture that to imagine separation seems ludicrous. How people view the world is influenced greatly by their cultural experience and basically defines much of who they are. Because of this influence, as counselors we must not only embrace the diversity of our client population but also embrace the diversity within ourselves and our field.

RESISTANCE TO THEORIES: ECLECTIC, INTEGRATED, OR JUST DON'T KNOW

Many beginning helping professionals do not subscribe to one specific theory but rather identify themselves as being eclectic or integrative. Evidence supports trends in this area. Many theory textbooks now include chapters that focus on eclectic and integrative approaches, such as Lazarus's (1989) multimodal theory and Prochaska and DiClemente's (1982) transtheoretical model, along with many others. This trend is further evidenced by surveys of mental health practitioners, who, when asked about their theoretical orientation, identify themselves as eclectic (Schmidt, 2001; Wrenn, 1960).

While it is plausible and pragmatic for clinicians to choose interventions from various schools of thought, this choice requires intentionality and a thorough working knowledge of the utilized theories. Sometimes, however, students endorse eclectic theories without having the required knowledge and intentionality of seasoned practitioners.

Although not always the case, portraying oneself as eclectic can be an "easy out" when one is asked about personal theory. We have heard several students say that, while interviewing for clinical positions, they present themselves as eclectic in an attempt to avoid presenting a theory not endorsed by the interviewer. These students believe that there is a "right" answer and that part of their interviewing success depends on their ability to show themselves as congruent with the interviewer or open to the interviewer's personal theory. As you likely can see, your theory is ultimately based on your life philosophy—*your* values and beliefs—which in many ways are highly personal. To offer a specific theory, a revelation of yourself, places you in a vulnerable position that portrays you and puts you in a place where judgment may occur. Especially as a beginning counselor, you may find it frightening to say specifically to which theory you ascribe. If you state, "I am a feminist therapist," you may be questioned about what that means, what your beliefs are, and what interventions a feminist helper utilizes in therapy. By identifying yourself as grounded in a specific theory, you are making both a statement about what you believe and who you are and a commitment to how you will work with clients. For example, if we say we are psychoanalytic therapists, you have the opportunity to make some assumptions about us. Consequently, some students feel safer saying, "I am eclectic."

Other students have shared that their portrayal as eclectic allowed them to utilize interventions that they believed would work. They shared that this allowed them to be "themselves" and to accept individual clients as they are. The helping professions do typically promote individuality, so this argument has some merit. If helpers do not orient themselves with a specific theory, however, they are not in a place where they can justify their work with clients. By not justifying their approach, they thereby circumvent truly intentional, ethical counseling.

An additional struggle with eclectic approaches revolves around the issue of student and clinical supervision. To train effective and ethical helpers, educators and supervisors must give counselors feedback on their clinical work. Typically, counselor educators and clinical supervisors attempt to provide counselors with feedback that is based on the supervisees' specific approach. When students and beginning counselors adopt an eclectic model, providing specific feedback is difficult. Not uncommonly, students and counselors endorse this paradigm of eclecticism to avoid targeted feedback. Students may do this not because they want to avoid learning or even grading but rather because they fear being evaluated as a helping professional.

This resistance to adopting a theoretical orientation can surface in many forms. While the purpose of this text is to help counselors dedicate themselves to a theory, it is also an attempt to advocate for the helping professions and increase the professionalism of their identities. For example, because of the impact of health-care reform and managed care, as a profession, we are constantly required to provide more justification for counseling and psychotherapy. If, as professionals, helpers are unable to portray themselves as being theory driven, they run the risk of being seen as incompetent and unreimbursable. Thus, each counselor's openness to having strong theoretical foundations adds to the professionalism of the counseling field.

DOES IT REALLY WORK?

Let us offer you an example where we supervised a counselor-in-training through a practicum experience. In this class, the students saw clients while we had the opportunity to observe them through a one-way mirror and make calls into the session to offer suggestions and reflections. The student we observed, Carolyn, showed a great level of understanding of theory, and she demonstrated skills beyond what is typical of her level of training. She consistently demonstrated the ability to develop quick rapport with her clients and was keenly attuned to the affective world of her clients.

She was working with a college student who was experiencing social anxiety and was potentially struggling with test anxiety. Carolyn was doing great work with her client and was really helping the client to see herself in a new way. In session, Carolyn was helping the client to examine what thoughts and events tend to trigger times of greatest anxiety. She was also sharing her observations of her client's social skills. Although the client was verbally expressing a fear of others, she was being quite open and honest with Carolyn. During the session, Carolyn also encouraged the client by saying that she "would be okay." A segment of the session follows.

Carolyn: So, during times where you notice you have values in common with others, you feel the greatest sense of social confidence.

Client: Well, I guess, but I still find I don't know how to talk with others. I struggle, as I don't feel I can be open with others. I am scared, frightened, and feel I have nothing to offer. I feel others will look at me and laugh and see how . . . well, how stupid I am. I am not quick and, well, because of this I don't talk. I try to keep the focus off of me.

Carolyn: So then you back down as you feel you have little to offer.

Client: Yes, I cannot be open with others. I have never been able to be honest with others about how I feel and stuff.

Carolyn: So you feel you really struggle opening up to others.

Client: Well, yes, all of the time.

Carolyn: What is hard for me to understand is how you believe you are never honest, yet you have been very honest with me today . . . you have shared your vulnerabilities without shutting down.

Client: Well . . . (smiling). Yeah, I guess. Maybe I am not always able to see when I am being open.

Carolyn: Sorta like, sometimes you are able to do it but don't see it.

Client: Yeah!

Carolyn: You know, I think you will be okay.

Following the session, we listened to Carolyn's reflections and gave her feedback. During this experience, we were shocked at Carolyn's appraisal of the session. Carolyn shared that she believed her statement, "You know, I think you will be okay," was the most beneficial during the session. In fact, however, this statement was the least grounded in theory. Carolyn went on to say that she felt that her statement, "What is hard for me to understand is how you believe you are never honest, yet you have been very honest with me today . . . you have shared your vulnerabilities without shutting down," was completely a value statement that would have been better not to share and did not have a place in counseling. We were again surprised by her appraisal—not only because Carolyn's statement was grounded in the existential approach's value of being authentic but also because the client later shared that it was the most meaningful interaction she encountered during her course of therapy. When we shared this discrepancy with Carolyn, she said, "But I am not a humanist." After exploration with Carolyn, we learned that she had adopted her theoretical approach based not on her philosophy or worldview but on, as she put it, "the theory my last supervisor liked."

During the following weeks, we asked Carolyn if she would take a step back from her theory. We asked her first to identify her values and philosophy of life. As she did, many themes emerged, and these focused greatly on her belief that people know what is best for themselves and that being genuine with others is essential to meaningful relationships. These perspectives are the cornerstones of many humanistic approaches, and these new insights helped Carolyn to begin to build a theory that would not only be effective with clients but also enable her to have a theoretical approach that truly fit for her. Through this process, she was able to find a theory that was more congruent with her values and a way to be theory driven while incorporating herself in the session. Carolyn's confidence and skill level with clients continued to increase. Clearly, in her work with clients, Carolyn's new confidence and self-understanding were increasing her effectiveness and ultimately helping her clients. Carolyn found that the humanistic approach was a natural for her to be effective with clients. She found that she could be grounded in a theory that was congruent with her beliefs and truly allowed her actions in therapy to be based on her values.

WHAT TO TAKE HOME

Each helper brings individual qualities to the therapeutic process. Your religion, ethnicity, gender, and sociological background contribute so much not only to who you are as a person but also to how you serve as a counselor. As an individual, how you interpret or make meaning of your experiences inevitably changes you. Your adoption of core values and beliefs affects not only you but also your clients. Your theoretical orientation can help you conceptualize and intervene with clients in a way that is effective for the client while staying congruent with who you are.

The process of adopting a theory that truly fits your own belief system is difficult—but very attainable. It is an ongoing process because new experiences continuously influence your beliefs and values. At times, learning more about yourself may even require you to give up what were once cardinal components of your counseling approach. Being a theory-based clinician is an ethical and essential step in a helper's development. Through self-inquiry and study, you can begin a journey that can help you to become an effective counselor whose actions not only are based in theory but also truly emanate from your own beliefs. Discovering your own values, life philosophy, and view of counseling and psychotherapy is an important step in your professional identity. However, you must also identify the views, values, and life philosophy of your clients.

Following the proposed ITS model is one pragmatic way for you to adopt a theory that is congruent with who you are. It offers you the opportunity to develop or hone your understanding and purposefulness of the goals you, and potentially your clients, choose in the therapeutic relationship. Theory offers you a framework for where to go in the counseling relationship. If goals are congruent with the counselor's theoretical orientation, then *what you do*—the selected techniques—in counseling should also be theoretically founded.

REFLECTION QUESTIONS

1. The following questions are designed to assist you as you begin to articulate your life philosophy: (a) What do you value? (b) What do you find meaningful? (c) What influences in your life have been most profound in shaping your life philosophy?

2. Of the six schools of thought described in the chapter (psychodynamic, behavioral, humanistic, pragmatic, constructivist, and family), which one(s) do you feel most knowledgeable about? Which one(s) would you like to learn more about?

3. Think of three clinical techniques you currently can use or know of (e.g., empty chair, free association, charting, education, confrontation, and so on). Can you identify the theory to which each technique belongs?

4. What do you consider to be your cultural background? How do you feel your cultural background affects your personal relationships? Your professional relationships?

5. In recent counseling and psychotherapy research, there has been a trend toward integrative and eclectic techniques. What about these approaches do you find attractive? What about these approaches do you find unattractive?

6. In examining the ITS model, identify the components (a) with which you feel confident and (b) for which you need additional education, information, and/or experience.

Word peace, allow people to
respect other people points of view,
go ahead afford

Top 10 Ways to Find Your Theoretical Orientation

3

Selecting your theoretical orientation in a purposeful manner requires both knowledge of counseling theories and self-knowledge. As presented earlier, learning about yourself and your own life philosophy is the first step in integrating a theory of counseling. The Intentional Theory Selection (ITS) model serves as a road map to finding your theoretical orientation. Finding your theoretical orientation requires you to be active in learning about yourself and how this information influences what theory might best fit for you.

In the style of a late-night show, we will give you the top 10 ways to find your theoretical orientation. We believe that each strategy can lead you closer to your theoretical orientation and that each is important in the overall process of developing your theoretical orientation.

1. Find yourself.
2. Articulate your values.
3. Survey your preferences.
4. Use your personality.
5. Capture yourself.
6. Let others inspire you in your learning.
7. Read original works.
8. Get real.
9. Study with a master.
10. Broaden your experiences.

We will discuss each of these top 10 methods in this chapter.

FIND YOURSELF

To choose a theoretical orientation that best fits you, you need to consider your own values, life philosophy, and worldview in an honest way. All helpers may aspire to provide unconditional positive regard and respect for clients, but the reality of clients' lives and behaviors may make that difficult to accomplish. Thus, we encourage you to be thoughtful and honest as you participate in the following activities, which are designed to help you examine your values. You may find journaling about your values and reactions to the following questions helpful.

1. *Who should go to counseling?* Ask yourself, "Who is counseling for?" Is it best for those who have major life traumas? Those who have "small problems"? Or perhaps for those whose problems are somewhere in between? Figuring out "who are our clients?" may be just as important as the process of figuring out "who are our counselors?"

2. *What would you want in a counselor?* Would you like a counselor who asked you lots of questions? Would you want a counselor who gave you lots of advice? What would you not want a counselor to do? Ponder the type of counselor you might want, and perhaps such thoughts will give you insight about your own theoretical orientation.

3. *What do you think should be the focus of therapy?* Should facts, feelings, or behaviors be the focus of therapy? Are therapists there to solve the client's problems, or should the client be in charge? Therapies and therapists vary greatly. What do you think is the basis of therapy?

4. *What do you think makes an effective counselor?* Should counselors be serious? Is there a place for humor in therapy? Should therapists share about themselves? Or should therapy be focused on the client? Is rapport a needed component of therapy? Should therapists have "experienced" problems to be a good problem solver?

5. *Should therapy consider spiritual or religious aspects?* If you answered yes to this question, do the spiritual beliefs of the therapist make a difference in therapy? Do you believe in free-will? Is morality an absolute or is it defined by the situation?

6. *What "causes us to be the way we are"?* The past, the present, or even the spiritual? Should therapy look at these factors? Therapy is often about fixing something or making something better. What you believe about how we get to our current state of affairs may affect what you see as valuable in therapy.

These questions will help you examine your values as they relate to the counseling process. As you think about the questions, write down your answers, which can help you identify your theoretical orientation. Your values, as they relate to the helping process, are just one way to examine yourself. To get a complete picture of your values as they relate to the helping process, you need to examine your counseling-related values and your personal values. You will examine your personal values more in the next step.

ARTICULATE YOUR VALUES

We have developed some questions to assist you in examining your values and life philosophy. To begin the journey of introspection and imagination that will lead you to uncover your own value system and life philosophy, consider your honest answers to the questions in the following scenarios.

■ *The Funeral.* Imagine that you have been transported through time to your own funeral, where your family and all the friends in your life have gathered. As part of the ceremony, an open microphone is provided for people who want to speak about their remembrances of you.

What do you think people would say about you? What would you like them to say?

caring, sarcastic, loving, adventorous

■ *Free Week.* Imagine that suddenly you have been given one magical week of "free" life—you do not have to take care of tasks at work, finances, family, and household responsibilities. No backlog would accumulate. You would reenter the year at exactly the same time you left it, but you would have seven days for yourself. It would be as though the calendar had 53 weeks, just for you.

What would you do? Who, if anyone, would you include?

travel!!!
with my loved ones

■ *Change.* Imagine that you have been given the power to change three things about yourself *permanently*.

What three things would you choose to change? Why?

reduce anxiety, love myself fully,
be present in the moment

What would you change in your neighborhood? In your town? In your city? Why?

clean up liter, affordable living,
mandatory Sundays off

What would you change if your power were extended to people in general? Why?

affordable costs of life, equality
for all, no violence

If your power were now extended to the world, what would you choose to change permanently? Why?

World peace, allow people to respect other people points of view, no social media

How do your views of multiculturalism and diversity relate to the details and ideas that you selected to change permanently about your city? About your state? About the world in which you live?

All people are equal and should be treated that way

Review your answers to the personal values questions, and then answer the following questions:

- What themes emerged from your answers?
- How are the changes that you strive for related to the changes that you hope your clients will make?
- What are your priorities?
- How are those priorities related to the way you work with clients?
- What kind of changes do you want to make for yourself and the world around you?
- How do these changes affect your role as a helping professional?

SURVEY YOUR PREFERENCES

Now that you have had a chance to reflect on your priorities and values as a person and as a professional, you can participate in a survey that we developed to help you determine your theoretical orientation. The Selective Theory Sorter–Revised (STS–R) survey items are based on a literature review of numerous important counseling books and articles (e.g., Corey, 2004; Doyle, 1998; Ivey & Ivey, 1999; Jackson & Thompson, 1971; Murdock, 2009; Nichols, 2008; Young, 1998). The survey is designed to give you insight into your theoretical preferences and assess your views of pathology, the counseling process, and treatment modalities. It is not designed to be a diagnostic tool; rather, it is another tool for your self-exploration. The STS–R appears on pages 31–36.

USE YOUR PERSONALITY

Your personality type can help to guide you toward a theoretical orientation. The Myers-Briggs Type Indicator (MBTI), a measure commonly used to examine personality characteristics, can be another way to help you to understand your way of viewing the world (Myers & Myers, 1977). If you do not know your Myers-Briggs type, you might find it helpful to take the test, which is typically offered at career services offices on college campuses.

SELECTIVE THEORY SORTER–REVISED

Read the following statements and indicate the strength of your beliefs in the white box following the statement. Your response for each item can range from −3 to +3 depending on the extent to which you believe a statement is not at all like you (−3) to a lot like you (+3). For example, if you believe the statement presented in item 30, "People are sexual beings," is a lot like your view of counseling, your answer might look like this:

	Not At All Like Me −3 −2 −1	Neutral 0	A Lot Like Me 1 2 3
30. People are sexual beings.			3

| | Not At All Like Me
−3 −2 −1 | | Neutral
0 | | A Lot Like Me
1 2 3 | |

	A	B	C	D	E	F	G	H	I	J	K	L
1. Individual problems are best viewed in the context of a family system.											1	
2. A major goal of therapy should be to assist the client in reaching a stage of unconditional self-acceptance by changing irrational beliefs.								2				
3. A warm relationship between the therapist and client is not a necessary or sufficient condition for effective personality change.								3				
4. Behavior is a way to control perceptions.									3			
5. Behavior is both consciously and unconsciously motivated by the environment and psychic energy.			3									
6. Childhood events are the baseline for adult personality.	1											
7. Childhood sexual attractions toward parents are responsible for later neurotic symptoms.	−3											
8. Clients are capable of imagining which behaviors are desirable and then working to make those images a behavioral reality.								1				

CHAPTER THREE

	A	B	C	D	E	F	G	H	I	J	K	L
9. Clients must take ultimate responsibility for the way their life is lived.												3
10. Coming to grips with the unconscious part of the personality is the only way to truly achieve individuation.			-2									
11. Dream interpretation, free association, hypnotic techniques, and fantasizing are good ways of gaining access to the client's unconscious.	-2											
12. Each person determines the essence of his or her existence.					3							
13. Each person is unique and has the ability to reach full potential.					3							
14. Everyone is unique.					3							
15. Counseling should include advocating for clients.							3					
16. Culture should be of utmost consideration in the counseling relationship.							3					
17. Goals of therapy should include assisting the clients in learning the consciousness of their responsibility, bringing unconscious spiritual factors to the conscious, and recovering meaning to existence.											3	
18. How a person thinks largely determines how that person feels and behaves.										3		
19. Human problems stem *not* from external events or situations *but* from people's views or beliefs about them.									0			
20. Humans are constantly striving to maintain equilibrium.					3							
21. Humans are pulled by the future and are self-controlled.		1										
22. Humans strive for actualization—to maintain or promote growth.				2								
23. Irrational beliefs are the principal cause of emotional disturbance.									0			
24. It is important to fulfill one's needs, and to do so in a way that does not deprive others of the ability to fulfill their needs.										3		

	A	B	C	D	E	F	G	H	I	J	K	L
25. Maladaptive behaviors, like adaptive behaviors, are learned. They can also be unlearned.							1					
26. Maladjusted behavior results in losing effective control over perceptions and over entire lives.									-1			
27. Gender is an important dynamic in the counseling relationship.					0							
28. Movement toward psychological growth and self-actualizing is often sabotaged by self-defeating thoughts.								3				
29. Mutual trust, acceptance, and spontaneity are important when building the counselor-client relationship.				3								
30. People are sexual beings.	3											
31. People control what they believe, not what actually exists.									2			
32. People have both internal and external definitions of themselves.									2			
33. People have the need to survive and reproduce—basic biological needs.				3								
34. Personality development is founded more on a progression of learned cognitions than on biological predispositions.										-3		
35. Personality is acquired through the use of negative and/or positive reinforcers.								2				
36. Personality is constructed through the attribution of meaning.												2
37. Providing genuineness, unconditional positive regard, and empathic understanding is essential to promote growth in the client.					3							
38. Recognizing cognitive processing in emotion and behavior is central in therapy.										3		
39. Social urges take precedence over sexual urges in personality development.		0										
40. Successful adaptation to life depends on the degree of social interest in goal striving.		1										

	A	B	C	D	E	F	G	H	I	J	K	L
41. The central focus of counseling should be the client's experiencing of feelings.				1								
42. The conscious rather than the unconscious is the primary source of ideas and values.		-1										
43. Therapy would be optimal if all impacted family members came into the counseling office together.											2	
44. Major therapeutic gains can occur in a short amount of time.						2						
45. The integration of the total person in his or her own unique field is essential in therapy.						3						
46. People's problems are best viewed as separate from themselves.						3						
47. The past determines the present, even though human motivation should be focused on the future.				1								
48. The process of individuation and self-realization should be the goal of living and of therapy.				2								
49. The purpose of therapy is to bring the unconscious to the conscious.	2											
50. The role in the family is one of the biggest influences in determining the personality characteristics of the client.			2									
51. The unconscious contains more than repressed material; it is a place of creativity, guidance, and meaning.				3								
52. The ways people form, organize, and interpret their basic cognitive structures determine how they will perceive and behave.										3		
53. Often individual problems occur due to the structure of one's immediate family.											2	
54. Therapy should be based in the here-and-now, where every moment of life matters.												3

TOP 10 WAYS TO FIND YOUR THEORETICAL ORIENTATION 35

	A	B	C	D	E	F	G	H	I	J	K	L
55. Therapy should focus on living more honestly and being less caught up in trivialities.												2
56. There are no underlying causes for maladjustment. Maladjustive behavior can be directly defined and attacked.							0					
57. Individual change occurs best by changing the family.											1	
58. Much of how we define ourselves comes from our family.											2	
59. There is no such thing as free will or voluntary behavior.							-3					
60. Viewing an event or situation out of context is one of the systematic errors in cognitive reasoning.										3		
Column Totals	3	3	11	16	15	11	0	3	6	9	8	13

SCORING THE SELECTIVE THEORY SORTER

1. Add the scores in each column. Be sure to add the positive numbers and subtract the negative numbers accurately. You may have scores below zero.
2. Transfer the column totals to the corresponding theories listed below.

   THEORY OR SCHOOL OF THOUGHT   **TOTAL SCORE**
   A. Psychoanalytic   3
   B. Analytic psychology   3
   C. Individual psychology   11
   D. Person-centered   16
   E. Gestalt   15
   F. Constructivist school of thought   11
   G. Behaviorism   0
   H. REBT   3
   I. Reality therapy   6
   J. Cognitive-behavioral   9
   K. Family theories school of thought   8
   L. Existential   13

3. Find the two or three theories or schools of thought with the highest scores and list them below. Based on your scores, these are the theories or schools of thought most appealing to you.

   THEORY OR SCHOOL OF THOUGHT   **TOTAL SCORE**
   person-centered   16 ⎫
   gestalt   15 ⎬ humanistic
   existential   13 ⎭
   individual / constructivist   11
   cbt   9

EXPLANATION OF SCORING

The STS–R is based on a comprehensive review of literature surrounding counseling theories. The items contained in the STS–R reflect the beliefs inherent in each theory or school of thought. Currently, no published psychometric properties are attached to the STS–R; however, the survey has been effective in tracking changes in individuals' theoretical orientation choice (Johnson & Halbur, 2013). Consequently, it is a survey that is intended for self-discovery.

The two or three theories or schools of thought you found most appealing and thus scored the highest are those that likely match your life philosophy as it is today; however, these are only preferences. For example, if you had two theories that tied, then you might need to examine and read about them in more depth. You may have also discovered that your preferences match a theory with which you are unfamiliar. Regardless of your results, you might find that looking in greater depth at the theories you identified gives you a better understanding of the theories and greater confidence in your ability to select one.

The theories corresponding to the constructivist and family schools of thought contain such great philosophical overlap that they are identified only as overall schools of thought. Consequently, their individual theories are not included in the STS–R. This is not intended to imply, however, that they are not as important.

Developed by Isabel Briggs Myers and Katherine Briggs in the 1950s, the MBTI is a forced-choice, self-report inventory that classifies individuals into 1 of 16 personality types, each with a unique set of characteristics and tendencies (Willis, 1989). Because the MBTI is theoretically conceptualized from a personal wellness rather than a pathology perspective, all the choices presented are seen as appropriate and acceptable ways of interacting with the environment and emphasize the traits or characteristics that support the balance of the individual's psychological personality system. According to Myers and McCaulley (1985), the main objective of the MBTI is to identify a combination of four basic preferences that determine type. An individual receives a four-letter code type determined by her scores on four theoretically independent dimensions. Each dimension has two dichotomous preferences, with only one preference from each dimension ascribed to any one individual (Willis, 1989).

The first dimension is the Extraversion/Introversion (E/I) index. The E/I index is designed to reflect whether a person is an extravert or an introvert. An *extravert* is defined as a person who directs energy and attention to the outer world and receives energy from external events, experiences, and interactions. An *introvert* prefers to focus on the inner world of ideas and impressions, thoughts, feelings, and reflections and draws energy from that process (Myers & McCaulley, 1998).

Sensing/iNtuition (S/N) is the second index. The S/N index reflects a person's preference between two opposite ways of perceiving, sensing or intuiting. A person who relies primarily on the process of sensing reports observable facts or happenings through one or more of the five senses. People with sensing preferences observe the world around them and are skilled at recognizing the practical realities of a situation. A person who responds more to intuition reports meanings, relationships, and/or possibilities and sees the big picture, focusing on connections, understandings, and relationships between facts (Myers & McCaulley, 1998).

The third dimension is the Thinking/Feeling (T/F) index. The T/F index describes a person's preference between two contrasting ways of making judgments. A person who typically reacts from a thinking perspective to make decisions on the basis of logical consequences or objective truth is identified as a thinking type. Thinking relies on principles of cause and effect and tends to be impersonal (Myers & McCaulley, 1985). People associated with thinking may develop characteristics associated with analytical ability, objectivity, and concern with justice and fairness. In contrast, a person who operates based on feeling makes decisions on the basis of personal or social values with the goal of harmony and recognition of the individual (Myers, 1993). Feeling-type people support their decisions with an understanding of personal values and group values, and thus they tend to be more subjective than thinking-type people. Feeling-type people also tend to be people-oriented and are characterized as having concern with the human, a need for affiliation, a capacity for warmth, and a desire for harmony (Myers & McCaulley, 1985).

The fourth dimension is the Judging/Perceiving (J/P) index. The J/P index describes the process that a person uses in dealing with the outer world—the extraverted part of life. Persons who prefer judgment use one of the judgment processes of thinking or feeling for dealing with the outside world. Perceiving types tend to operate from a sensing or an intuition perspective when dealing with the outside world.

Because counselors tend to select counseling theories that fit their own personality styles, you may find research regarding the MBTI and theoretical orientation helpful in your quest for a theoretical orientation (Erickson, 1993). The Thinking/Feeling preference on the MBTI is particularly illuminating when examining theoretical orientation. Thinking types tend to interact with others in a task-oriented, analytic, and objective manner. Feeling types tend to focus on personal values, subjective viewpoints, and people-oriented discussions. Thus, thinking types are disproportionately likely to choose predominantly cognitive theories such as Adlerian therapy, behavioral therapy, rational emotive behavioral therapy (REBT), and reality therapy. Feeling types are more likely to choose predominantly affective theories such as Gestalt, existential, and client-centered therapy.

Taking the MBTI

[handwritten: ISTJ: introvert, sensing, think, judge]

A number of resources allow counselors to take the MBTI. Counselors, consultants, and other human services professionals may offer this test as a professional service. Counseling students may be afforded the opportunity to take the test as part of their academic coursework and/or through their institution's counseling center. Though the MBTI is recommended in this text, many other personality inventories may be helpful to you in your mission of self-discovery. We chose the MBTI because it has been researched in relation to theory selection among counselors and psychotherapists.

CAPTURE YOURSELF

Audio, digital, and video recording techniques are valuable ways to capture yourself working as a professional helper. Recording techniques can show you whether or not your counseling skills actually convey your theory. The theoretical orientation you espouse should be one that is easily recognizable on recordings so that you can determine whether your interventions, strategies, and ways of relating to your clients are congruent with your theoretical orientation. Sometimes, viewing themselves on a recording is the first time students in the helping professions recognize that their intended theoretical orientation is not apparent in the counseling session. Thus, observing yourself can help you track your progress toward intentional counseling and use of theory in the helping relationship. Recording yourself also provides an opportunity for you to receive feedback from others who can assist you in understanding whether or not your clinical work is reflective of the theoretical orientation you espouse.

LET OTHERS INSPIRE YOU IN YOUR LEARNING

Others can inspire you in your learning in many ways. This text, which gives you an opportunity to examine your theoretical orientation, is a launching pad for exploring your role as a professional helper. Professional conferences and other professional development opportunities that you can attend may also help. The most well-regarded people in the field often conduct workshops that can help you understand theory and therapeutic techniques better. To get involved in these educational opportunities, ask your faculty members, supervisors, and colleagues about the professional organizations to which they belong. You can find numerous professional growth opportunities at the state, regional, national, and international levels.

READ ORIGINAL WORKS

Theories textbooks offer a wealth of information about various theories. Each time a theory is paraphrased, however, something is lost. Thus, we recommend that you read as many works by the original theorists as possible. The list of suggested readings and webpages at the end of the chapter is organized around the six schools of thought and their theories, which are presented in Chapter 4. The list is not all-encompassing; it is simply intended to get you started. Reading the words of the theorists gives you additional insight into the values they espoused or hold and the philosophy of their theories, which helps you to see which are congruent with your own life philosophy.

GET REAL

Another way you can solidify your theoretical orientation is to put it to the test with some real-world trials. As you conduct the activities of your everyday life, try your theoretical orientation with people in all sorts of situations and backgrounds. For example, one professional counselor had what she called a "typical Saturday." She spent her day going to the grocery store, getting a haircut, and attending a cultural event. The counselor reported that, while getting her hair cut, she interacted with a 20-year-old Caucasian hairdresser who was expecting her second child and was unsure of her relationship with the child's father. At the grocery store, the counselor interacted with a cashier in a wheelchair, and later she met a Bosnian house painter who was a highly regarded artist in Bosnia before the Bosnian War. In each of these situations, the counselor had the opportunity to monitor whether or not her humanistic leanings worked in her everyday life. The counselor noticed that she was able to have unconditional, positive regard for each of the people with whom she interacted. She also noted that she was not able to be genuine with each person she encountered but decided that her response was okay because each of these relationships was not a personal or counseling relationship. The counselor's experience illustrates the importance of finding a theoretical orientation that fits your personality. Because the theoretical orientation you espouse will ideally resonate with your being in most situations, you need one that fits with who you are both inside and outside the therapeutic relationship.

STUDY WITH A MASTER

One of the best ways to learn a theoretical approach to the helping professions is to study with a master or at an institute specializing in the theory in which you are interested. These opportunities will allow you to study with the creator of the theory or with some of the creator's protégés. Regardless of how you obtain additional education about a specific theory, that education will help you establish a theoretical orientation that fits for you. You can find many training opportunities both inside and outside the United States. Although you would need an immense amount of time to study at all institutes, you can pick experiences that are most appealing to you by reading original works and learning more about yourself. The following websites contain information that can get you started.

Albert Ellis Institute: rebt.org
American Association of Marriage and Family Therapy: aamft.org
Association for Humanistic Psychology: ahpweb.org
Association for Multicultural Counseling and Development: multicultural-counseling.org
→ Association for the Advancement of Gestalt Therapy: aagt.org
Beck Institute for Cognitive Therapy and Research: beckinstitute.org
→ Center for the Studies of the Person (Person-Centered): centerfortheperson.org
International Network on Personal Meaning (Existential): meaning.ca
Jean Baker Miller Training Institute (Feminist): jbmti.org
Mental Research Institute (Strategic/Brief): mri.org
Minuchin Center for the Family (Structural): minuchincenter.org
Narrative Therapy: narrativeapproaches.com
National Multicultural Institute: nmci.org
The Rollo May Center for Humanistic Studies: saybrook.edu
→ Solution-Focused Brief Therapy Association: sfbta.org
Viktor Frankl Institute of Logotherapy: logotherapyinstitute.org
William Glasser Institute: wglasser.com

BROADEN YOUR EXPERIENCES

The best way to expose yourself to new ideas and situations is by living outside your comfort zone, which may entail learning about cultures different from your own. Experiences outside your comfort zone not only allow you to encounter diverse thoughts but also allow you to compare your own beliefs to those unique to others. This may help you in articulating your worldview and anchoring your beliefs in cultures around you. To accomplish this, you may need to work with and experience a variety of clients' issues, which you can do in several ways. First, try to get experience working in a wide variety of settings. Spend time working with people of ethnicities, cultural backgrounds, and socioeconomic statuses that are different from your own. For example, if you are a mental health or community counselor, spend time working with adults, children, and families to expose yourself to as many diverse experiences as possible. If you are a school counselor, you may choose to get experience working with elementary, middle school, and high school students, ideally in schools that are different from one another.

Second, you may want to study abroad. Valuable opportunities to learn about counseling and other cultures are available through many graduate programs that offer multicultural and theories courses in other countries. You might seek grants such as a Fulbright scholarship to study the helping professions in another country. You can also have multicultural experiences without leaving the country. Many universities have organized international student groups where you can volunteer to be a conversation partner or to host an international student. These opportunities can add diversity to your day-to-day life.

TOP 10 WRAP-UP

The helping professions are unique compared to many other fields because self-understanding is essential to a job well done. To be an effective therapist, you must have a working theory to guide how you serve clients. Self-insight is the first step in the process of finding a theoretical orientation, and the key to finding your theoretical orientation is understanding your life philosophy. A few of the ways to gain greater self-understanding include finding your values, understanding your preferences, and having new experiences.

Engaging in activities that help you with personal insight can make you a better professional, which consequently contributes to your effectiveness in your work with clients. Your intentionality will ultimately help you to find a theory that is congruent with your values not only as a professional but also as a person. This will likely lead to a career you find more fulfilling.

In Chapter 4, we present some theories and explain how they fit with the ITS model. In Chapter 5, we provide some examples of students, clinicians, and supervisors who utilized the ITS model to aid them in their professional development. These individuals, diverse like the clients they now serve, went through the universal struggles that are common among those beginning in the helping field. We hope their experiences will help you in your own process.

REFLECTION QUESTIONS

1. In this chapter, you were asked to complete some exercises to articulate your values. What did you learn about yourself? How will you integrate your learning into your quest for a theoretical orientation?
2. After reviewing your results on the STS–R, which theories or schools of thought did you find most appealing? Least appealing? What are your thoughts on your results?
3. How does your cultural background affect the values you have?
4. How do your current theories of choice match with your personality or MBTI type?
5. Evaluate one of your counseling sessions on a video or audio recording. How do your skills demonstrate your current theoretical orientation? In what areas do you need improvement? Who can you ask to assist you in making sure that your skills match your stated theoretical orientation?
6. In your search to ascertain a theoretical orientation, which original works do you plan to read? Which opportunities to study with a master are most appealing to you? How will you obtain these experiences? When?

SUGGESTED READINGS AND WEBPAGES

PSYCHODYNAMIC APPROACHES

Psychoanalytic Theory

Freud, S. (1966). *A general introduction to psychoanalysis*. New York, NY: W. W. Norton. (Original work published 1920)
Freud, S., & Strachey, J. (Ed.). (1983). *Interpretation of dreams*. Asheville, NC: Avon.
Freud, S., Strachey, J., & Gay, P. (1975). *Group psychology and the analysis of the ego*. New York, NY: W. W. Norton.
Freud, S., Strachey, J., & Gay, P. (1990). *Beyond the pleasure principle*. New York, NY: W. W. Norton.
American Psychoanalytic Association (APsaA)—apsa.org
Division of Psychoanalysis (Division 39) of the American Psychological Association—division39.org
Institute of Psychoanalysis (British Psychoanalytical Society)—psychoanalysis.org.uk
International Psychoanalytic Association—ipa.org.uk/
Psychoanalytic Electronic Publishing—pep-web.org

Individual Psychology

Adler, A. (1998). *What life could mean to you*. Center City, MN: Hazelden Information Education.
Adler, A., Ansbacher, H. L., & Ansbacher, R. R. (1989). *The Individual Psychology of Alfred Adler: A systematic presentation in selections from his writings*. New York, NY: HarperCollins.
Adler Graduate School (AGS)—alfredadler.edu
International Association of Individual Psychology (IAIP)—iaipwebsite.org
North American Society of Adlerian Psychology (NASAP)—alfredadler.org

Analytical Theory

Jung, C. (1958). *Psychology and religion*. New York, NY: Pantheon.
Jung, C. (1965). *Memories, dreams, reflections*. New York, NY: Vintage Books.
Archive for Research in Archetypal Symbolism (ARAS)—aras.org
Jung Page —cgjungpage.org
New York Association for Analytical Psychology (NYAAP)—nyaap.org

BEHAVIORISM

Skinner, B. F. (1976). *About behaviorism*. New York, NY: Random House.
Skinner, B. F. (1976). *Walden two*. Boston, MA: Pearson.

Skinner, B. F. (2002). *Beyond freedom and dignity*. Indianapolis, IN: Hackett.
Association for Behavioral and Cognitive Therapies (ABCT)—abct.org

HUMANISTIC PPROACHES

Person-Centered

Rogers, C. (1951). *Client-centered therapy: Its current practice, implications, and theory*. Boston, MA: Houghton Mifflin.
Rogers, C. (1957). The necessary and sufficient conditions of therapeutic personality change. *Journal of Consulting Psychology, 21*, 95–103.
Rogers, C. (1961). *On becoming a person*. Boston, MA: Houghton Mifflin.
Rogers, C. (1969). *Freedom to learn*. Columbus, OH: Merrill.
Rogers, C. (1970). *On encounter groups*. New York, NY: HarperCollins.
Rogers, C. (1972). *Becoming partners*. New York, NY: Delta.
Rogers, C. (1977). *On personal power*. New York, NY: Delacourt.
Rogers, C. (1980). *A way of being*. Boston, MA: Houghton Mifflin.
Rogers, C. (1995). *On becoming a person: A therapist's view of psychotherapy*. Boston, MA: Houghton Mifflin.
Rogers, C., & Wallen, J. (1946). *Counseling with returned servicemen*. New York, NY: McGraw-Hill.
Association for Humanistic Psychology (AHP)—ahpweb.org
Center for Studies of the Person (CSP)—centerfortheperson.org
International Network of Personal Meaning (INPM)—meaning.ca
Saybrook Graduate School—Research Center—saybrook.edu

Existential

Frankl, V. (1967). *Psychotherapy and existentialism: Selected papers on Logotherapy*. New York, NY: Washington Square Press.
Frankl, V. (1969). *The will to meaning*. New York, NY: New American Library.
Frankl, V. (1985). Logos, paradox, and the search for meaning. In M. J. Mahoney & A. Freeman (Eds.), *Cognition and psychotherapy* (pp. 259–275). New York, NY: Plenum.
Frankl, V. (1985). *The unheard cry for meaning: Psychotherapy and humanism*. New York, NY: Simon & Schuster.
Frankl, V. (1992). *Man's search for meaning: An introduction to Logotherapy* (3rd ed.). New York, NY: Oxford University Press.
Maslow, A. (1962). *Toward a psychology of being*. New York, NY: Van Nostrand.
Maslow, A. (1971). *The farther reaches of human nature*. New York, NY: Viking.
May, R. (1958). The origins and significance of the existential movement in psychology. In R. May, E. Angel, & H. Ellenberger (Eds.), *Existence* (pp. 3–36). New York, NY: Basic Books.
May, R. (Ed.). (1961). *Existential psychology*. New York, NY: Random House.
May, R. (1969). *Love and will*. New York, NY: W. W. Norton.
May, R. (1983). *The discovery of being: Writings in existential psychology*. New York, NY: W. W. Norton.
May, R. (1992). *The art of counseling*. London, England: Souvenir Press. (Original work published 1939)
Yalom, I. D. (1980). *Existential psychotherapy*. New York, NY: Basic Books.
Yalom, I. D. (1990). *Love's executioner and other tales of psychotherapy*. New York, NY: Basic Books.
Yalom, I. D. (2001). *The gift of therapy*. New York, NY: HarperCollins.
Existential-Humanistic Institute (EHI)—ehinstitute.org
Existential Psychotherapy—existentialpsychotherapy.net
PsychAlive—psychalive.org
Society for Existential Analysis (SEA)—existentialanalysis.co.uk

Gestalt

Perls, F. (1969). *Gestalt therapy verbatim*. Moab, UT: Real People's Press.
Perls, F. (1969). *In and out of the garbage pail*. Moab, UT: Real People's Press.
Perls, F. (1973). *The Gestalt approach and eye witness to therapy*. Palo Alto, CA: Science & Behavior Books.
Association for the Advancement of Gestalt Therapy (AAGT)—aagt.org
Gestalt Review—gisc.org

Gestalt Therapy Network (GTN)—gestalttherapy.net
New York Institute for Gestalt Therapy (NYIGT)—newyorkgestalt.org

PRAGMATIC APPROACHES

Cognitive Behavioral

Beck, A. T. (1976). *Cognitive therapy and the emotional disorders.* New York, NY: International Universities Press.
Beck, A. (1991). Cognitive therapy: A 30-year retrospective. *American Psychologist, 46,* 368–375.
Beck, J. S., & Beck, A. T. (1995). *Cognitive therapy: Basics and beyond.* New York, NY: Guilford Press.
Burns, D. D. (1999). *Feeling good: The new mood therapy.* New York, NY: Wholecare.
Burns, D. D. (1999). *The feeling good handbook.* New York, NY: Plume.
Kelly, G. (1955). *The psychology of personal constructs* (Vols. 1 & 2). New York, NY: W. W. Norton.
Meichenbaum, D. (1977). *Cognitive-behavior modification: An integrative approach.* New York, NY: Plenum Press.
Meichenbaum, D. (1985). *Stress inoculation training.* Boston, MA: Allyn & Bacon.
Beck Institute for Cognitive Therapy and Research—beckinstitute.org
Center for Cognitive Therapy, University of Pennsylvania Health System—med.upenn.edu/cct
Cognitive Therapy Associates (CTA)—cognitive-therapy-associates.com/therapy/cognitive
International Association for Cognitive Psychotherapy (IACP)—the-iacp.com
National Association of Cognitive Behavioral Therapists (NACBT)—nacbt.org

Rational Emotive Behavioral Therapy

Ellis, A. (1971). *Growth through reason.* Palo Alto, CA: Science & Behavior Books.
Ellis, A. (1983). The origins of rational-emotive therapy (RET). *Voices, 18,* 29–33.
Ellis, A. (1994). *Reason and emotion in psychotherapy.* New York, NY: Birch Lane.
Ellis, A. (1995). Changing rational-emotive therapy to rational-emotive behavior therapy. *Journal of Rational-Emotive and Cognitive-Behavior Therapy, 13,* 85–90.
Ellis, A. (1996). *Reason and emotion in psychotherapy.* New York, NY: Carol Publishing Group.
Ellis, A. (1998). *How to make yourself happy and remarkably less disturbable.* San Luis Obispo, CA: Impact.
Ellis, A. (1999). Rational-emotive behavior therapy as an internal control psychology. *International Journal of Reality Therapy, 19,* 4–11.
Ellis, A. (2000). A continuation of the dialogue on issues in counseling in the postmodern era. *Journal of Mental Health Counseling, 22,* 97–106.
Albert Ellis Institute (AEI)—rebt.org
Rational Emotive Behavioral Therapy (REBT)—rebtnetwork.org
Self-Management and Recovery Training (SMART)—smartrecovery.org

Reality Therapy

Glasser, W. (1965). *Reality therapy.* New York, NY: HarperCollins.
Glasser, W. (1998). *Choice theory: A new psychology of personal freedom.* New York, NY: HarperPerennial.
Wubbolding, R. E. (2000). *Reality therapy for the 21st century.* Philadelphia, PA: Brunner Routledge.
Center for Reality Therapy—realitytherapywub.com
William Glasser Institute —wglasser.com

CONSTRUCTIVIST APPROACHES

Multicultural Counseling and Therapy

Atkinson, D., Morten, G., & Sue, D. W. (1997). *Counseling American minorities.* New York, NY: McGraw-Hill.
Pontorotto, J., Casas, J. M., Suzuki, L. A., & Alexander, C. (2001). *Handbook of multicultural counseling.* Thousand Oaks, CA: Sage.
Sue, D. W. (2003). *Overcoming our racism: The journey to liberation.* New York, NY: John Wiley.
Sue, D. W., & Sue, D. (2003). *Counseling the culturally diverse: Theory and practice.* New York, NY: John Wiley.
Association for Multicultural Counseling and Development (AMCD)—multiculturalcounseling.org

International MultiCultural Institute (iMCI)—imciglobal.org
National Guidance Research Forum (NGRF)—guidance-research.org/EG/impprac/ImpP2/new-theories/mcc

Feminist Approaches

Enns, C. Z. (1993). Twenty years of feminist counseling and therapy: From naming biases to implementing multi-faceted practice. *Counseling Psychologist, 21*(1), 3–87.
Gilligan, C. (1993). *In a different voice: Psychological theory and women's development.* Cambridge, MA: Harvard University Press.
Miller, J. B. (Ed.). (1973). *Psychoanalysis and women.* Baltimore, MD: Penguin Books.
Miller, J. B. (1976). *Toward a new psychology of women.* Boston, MA: Beacon Press.
Miller, J. B., & Stiver, I. P. (1997). *The healing connection: How women form relationships in therapy and in life.* Boston, MA: Beacon Press.
Miller, J. B., & Welch, A. S. (1995). Learning from women. In P. Chesler, E. D. Rothblum, & E. Cole (Eds.), *Feminist foremothers in women's studies, psychology, and mental health* (pp. 335–346). New York, NY: Haworth Press.
Association for Women in Psychology—awpsych.org
Jean Baker Miller Training Institute—jbmti.org
Society for the Psychology of Women / Division 35 of the American Psychological Association—apa.org/divisions/div35

Narrative Therapy

White, M. (2007). *Maps of narrative therapy.* New York, NY: W. W. Norton.
White, M., & Epston, D. (1990). *Narrative means to therapeutic ends.* New York, NY: W. W. Norton.
Center for Narrative Practice—narrativepractice.com
Institute of Narrative Therapy (INT)—theinstituteofnarrativetherapy.com
Narrative Therapy—narrativeapproaches.com
Narrative Therapy Centre of Toronto—narrativetherapycentre.com

Solution-Focused Brief Therapy

Berg, K. B. (2003). *Children's solution work.* New York, NY: W. W. Norton.
De Shazer, S. (1985). *Keys to solution in brief therapy.* New York, NY: W. W. Norton.
BRIEF / Brief Therapy Practice—brieftherapy.org.uk
Solution Focused Brief Therapy Association (SFBTA)—sfbta.org/

FAMILY APPROACHES

Bowen Family Systems Therapy

Giat Roberto, L. (1992). *Transgenerational family therapies.* New York, NY: Guilford Press.
Lieberman, S. (1979). *Transgenerational family therapy.* London, England: Croom Helm.
Bowen Center for the Study of the Family—thebowencenter.org
Living Systems—livingsystems.ca

Strategic Family Therapy

Haley, J., & Richeport-Haley, M. (2003). *The art of strategic therapy.* New York, NY: Brunner-Routledge.
Madanes, C. (1981). *Strategic family therapy.* San Francisco, CA: Jossey-Bass.
Jay Haley on Therapy—jay-haley-on-therapy.com
Mental Research Institute—mri.org/strategic_family_therapy.html
Strategic Family Therapy—psychpage.com/learning/library/counseling/strategic

Structural Family Therapy

Minuchin, S. (1974). *Families and family therapy.* Cambridge, MA: Harvard University Press.
Minuchin, S., & Fishman, H. C. (1981). *Family therapy techniques.* Cambridge, MA: Harvard University Press.
Minuchin Center for the Family (MCF)—minuchincenter.org

Six Schools of Thought and Their Theories of Helping

4

We hope you now have an understanding of how the Intentional Theory Selection (ITS) model can help you incorporate your theoretical orientation into practice. You may have also begun to see how your values affect your choice of a theoretical orientation and to consider how these values may influence your role as a helping professional. We now present six schools of related thought along with specific theories that often serve as the icons for each school. We have chosen to present a sample of those theories most commonly addressed in the literature. These theories are most commonly included in counseling training comprehensive exams and national examinations for counselor licensure. Each theory is presented in the format of the ITS model. The schools are presented as separate, discrete schools. It is important to remember, however, that there is crossover in the fundamental values, goals, and even techniques across the six schools of thought.

Each school will be outlined in a general overview. Then the philosophy, goals, and techniques, as well as comments on the application to diversity, of each specific theory are offered, serving as a summary of that theory's key components and the actions it suggests for working with clients. One example of a person's ITS is also shown within each school of thought. This will allow you to see how a sampling of counselors and psychotherapists would view the development of their own theoretical orientations.

This chapter is meant to serve either as a reminder of the main components of various theories to which you have been exposed or as a primer enticing you to look further at theories you may not completely understand. As was stated in Chapter 3, you can gain a greater appreciation and understanding of specific theories in many ways. Processes such as reading original works, surveying your preferences through tools such as the Selective Theory Sorter–Revised (STS–R), and studying with a master can provide you with the depth of understanding you need or want to truly integrate your own theoretical orientation and to help clients in a therapeutic setting.

TABLE 4.1 ITS-Style Summary of Theories

THEORY	PHILOSOPHY OF PEOPLE	SCHOOL	MAJOR THEORISTS	GOALS	COMMON TECHNIQUES
Psychoanalytic	Humans are sexual, hedonistic, and pleasure seeking; the unconscious is key to behavior; deconstructive; deterministic; developmental	Psychodynamic	Sigmund Freud; Anna Freud; Karen Horney	Insight; understanding; moving through past hurts; uncovering the unconscious	Free association; dream analysis; interpretation; analysis of transference
Analytical Psychology	Humans are connected ancestrally; holistic; spiritual; lifelong development; biological drives are important	Psychodynamic	Carl Jung	Individuation of the self; analysis of the psyche; archetypal understanding; personality integration	Insight; education; warm relationship; catharsis; dream analysis; archetypal analysis
Individual Psychology	Humans are social beings; holistic view of people; all behavior is goal-directed; people have free will and are creative	Psychodynamic	Alfred Adler	Increase social interest; understanding of personal private logic and goals	Therapeutic alliance; learning about client's lifestyle; collecting early recollections
Behavioral	Empirical; behavior is an environmental product; present-focused; scientific; people are hedonistic	Behavioral	B. F. Skinner	Environmental change; specific behavioral change	Education; reinforcement scheduling; modeling; systematic desensitization; relaxation techniques; assertiveness and skills training; charting; aversion therapy
Person-Centered	Humans strive to self-actualize; phenomenological; present is important	Humanistic	Carl Rogers	Self-actualization; increased congruence	Genuineness; unconditional positive regard; empathy
Existential	Finding life meaning is important; anxiety is based on core life conditions; people are free; phenomenological	Humanistic	Viktor Frankl; Irvin Yalom	Awareness; self-actualization; increased responsibility; acceptance of core conditions of life; create/find meaning in life	Relationship based; empathy; client understanding; meaning identification
Gestalt	Holistic; future-focused; experiential	Humanistic	Fritz Perls	Integration; increased self-responsibility	Awareness; empty chair; use of pronouns; sharing hunches; dream work
Cognitive-Behavioral Therapy	Thinking and feeling are connected; people are creative	Pragmatic	Aaron Beck; David Burns; Donald Meichenbaum	Changed thinking; identification of beliefs; awareness of automatic thoughts	Psychoeducation; collaborative relationship; behavioral techniques; cognitive modification

Theory	Key Concepts	Category	Founders	Goals	Techniques
REBT	Humans have an innate tendency toward actualization; tendency to focus on irrational thoughts	Pragmatic	Albert Ellis	Changed thinking; reduced irrational thoughts; changed value system	Education; confrontation; disputing irrational beliefs; homework; skill training
Reality Therapy	Humans strive to have needs met; all need survival, belonging, power, freedom, and fun	Pragmatic	William Glasser; Robert E. Wubbolding	Effective choices; acceptance of responsibility; understanding	Supportive relationships; contracts; create plans; pinning down; positive addicting behaviors; WDEP system
Multicultural Counseling	Culture-based; belief systems are important; problems may be external and culturally based	Constructivist	Derald Wing Sue; David Sue; Paul Pedersen; Patricia Arredondo	Cultural understanding; awareness of values and biases; understanding; change in oppressive systems	Worldview consideration; self-awareness; techniques vary based on client population
Feminist Theory	Oppressive systems contribute to women's psychosocial struggles; view women as positive	Constructivist	J. B. Miller; Carol Gilligan	Ability of client to see the world in various ways; deconstruction of traditional patriarchal culture	Egalitarian relationship; resource utilization; information sharing; personal validation challenging stereotypes; assertiveness training; advocacy
Narrative Therapy	People define themselves through stories; people are social; social constructivists; people have good intentions	Constructivist	Michael White	Changed thinking and living; use of positive stories to define self	Collaborative relationship; finding exceptions; authoring new stories; increasing choices; externalization storytelling; metaphors
Solution-Focused Brief Therapy (SFBT)	Change may occur in a short time; future-based; phenomenological	Constructivist	Insoo Kim Berg; Steve de Shazer	Identification of and action to solve problems; identification of the ways problems are maintained	Miracle questions; finding exceptions; strength assessment
Bowen Family Therapy	Family as an emotional unit; multigenerational	Family Approaches	Murray Bowen	Increased differentiation (similar to autonomy) of family members; lowered family anxiety and turmoil	Family assessment; therapist objectivity; genograms; sharing hypotheses
Strategic Family Therapy	Families perpetuate their problems; change can be sudden; creativity in change is important; therapy should focus on solutions	Family Approaches	Jay Haley; Milton Erikson; Cloé Madanes	Change in repetitive family patterns; learning what solutions have been attempted before	Paradoxical interventions; directives; prescribing the symptom; reframing; pretend techniques
Structural Family Therapy	Psychological illness is viewed as family issue, not individual issue; families need appropriate hierarchy; family has subsystems	Family Approaches	Salvador Minuchin	Definition of general boundaries; appropriate alignments; power adjustments; boundary clarity; changed transactional patterns	Joining; accommodating; family mapping; boundary making; unbalancing; enactment; reframing

The authors of this text have identified over 250 potential theories of counseling and psychotherapy. In addition, there are a multitude of approaches, some empirically validated, that at times are presented as comprehensive theories (see Chapter 2). Each theory has its unique strengths and limitations, and relevance to diverse populations; many theories stand alone as a useful paradigm for client conceptualization and as a guide for therapeutic intervention. However, individual approaches often have much in common with other theories and may look very similar. Consequently, each theory fits into a family, or a *school of thought*. Within each school of thought, the specific theories presented have related beliefs, with each individual theory looking more or less like the others. The six schools presented in this chapter are the psychodynamic, behavioral, humanistic, pragmatic, constructivist, and family approaches. See Table 4.1 for a summary of each theory; the table follows the ITS model.

PSYCHODYNAMIC SCHOOL OF THOUGHT

The first school of thought, and the one with the longest history, is the psychodynamic school of thought. In general, it views human beings as basically driven by psychic energy and molded by early experiences. Unconscious motives and conflicts are central in current presenting behavior. These psychic forces are strong, and individuals are thought to be driven by basic inherent impulses. Traditional psychoanalytic theory (primarily as developed by Sigmund Freud) views these impulses as solely sexual and aggressive. However, later theorists find strong motivations in other areas, such as socialization and individuation (a process of becoming whole). Development is of critical importance in psychodynamic approaches because later personality problems are believed to be rooted in childhood experiences.

The view of therapy in both the traditional and later approaches is typically based on a complex understanding of the personality, or the *psyche*. Each of these approaches looks deeply at what defines human experience and, with a few exceptions, what the structures of the personality are.

Therapeutic techniques are highly experiential and are typically considered to promote long-term, lifelong change. Change is rooted deeply in human nature and focused on insight and understanding. The therapeutic relationship is considered important. However, the insights offered are the primary precursors to change. The three primary theories of the psychodynamic approach are *psychoanalytic theory*, *analytical theory*, and *individual psychology*.

Psychoanalytic Theory

Sigmund Freud is often considered the founding father of psychotherapy. Freud lived in a time when medical intervention was the basis of psychological treatment. However, he increased the availability and recognition of talk therapy. Even in the layperson's world, Freud is known for identifying everything from slips of the tongue to defense mechanisms. To paint even a small picture of Freud would take a lot of canvas to express his many layers and complexities; only a few highlights are offered here.

Life Philosophy. Freud viewed the human world as filled with sexual impulses and deterministic ebbs. Freud basically believed that people struggle to balance complete animalistic and innate pleasure-seeking impulses with the challenges of social constraints (Gilliland & James, 1998). In addition, Freud believed that people must balance their repressed sexual and aggressive urges in order to feel and function in a healthy way.

Most of what people do is powered by *libidinal energy* that is hidden deep in their unconscious. This libidinal energy is dynamic in that it moves from various areas of the conscious and the unconscious, and it is limited. This energy, which is primarily sexual and aggressive, drives people's actions. However, most motivations and desires are beneath one's conscious awareness. Consequently, more often than not, when people experience psychological pain, they may not even know why. Freud believed that it was nearly impossible to directly "see" what is unconscious.

Freud was a deconstructivist; he broke the mind down into parts that played different roles in psychological functioning. He viewed the mind as having three structural divisions. At the most basic, primal level, he identified the *id*. The id, powered by the *pleasure principle*, is one's internal, biological baby who wants to be fed and have all needs—including eating, sleeping, and sex—met at all times. The *ego*, however, works on the *reality principle*, attempting to deal with a social world with limited resources. The ego also serves as the mediator between the id and the moralistic *superego*. The superego strives to be perfect and is one's personal, moralistic component. Conflict often occurs among these structural components of the mind, and these components of a person's mind drive every behavior. However, each component has a developmental beginning. For example, the superego does not emerge at birth but develops as a person receives messages of right and wrong, typically from parents. Children's egos develop as they learn that they live in a world of limited resources (e.g., food arrives only when adults deliver it). And one's id, which is present at birth, is innate and wants its needs met from day one.

As mentioned, psychoanalysis has a deterministic view of life. Nothing happens without a reason, and the past causes our behaviors. Consequently, human personality is determined by early childhood experience. Freud identified specific *psychosexual stages* that all people experience. As people develop, what happens around them ultimately happens to them. People mature and move through developmental stages and are met with challenges along the way. If they move through and meet these challenges successfully, they will typically maintain a relative level of health. If their struggles are too great, however, they may always be slightly stuck at one stage or, at the extreme, become fixated at an early psychosocial stage. At each stage, people focus on hedonistic gratification. This primarily sexual gratification is a developmental stage: getting one's needs met (gratification) and the process by which this occurs. At each step of the way, people run the risk of being psychologically traumatized. To avoid psychological fear and pain, people often take experiences, fluid in their conscious mind, and push them deep down in their unconscious mind. These experiences remain in the mind, however, hidden by *defense mechanisms*. Defenses, such as projection and repression, keep traumatic thoughts and emotions from infecting people's conscious lives. However, defense mechanisms do not banish fearful thoughts but merely keep them hidden. If the defense mechanisms do not work, however, finding a good therapist may be necessary.

The Psychosexual Stages. *Oral Stage (0–1).* The earliest psychosexual stage begins at birth. From birth to about one year of age, gratification comes orally. Chewing, biting, nursing, and eating become the sole forms of gratification. Babies innately respond to a mother's nipple or bottle, which becomes their first way to get their needs met. At this stage, babies already struggle because their oral needs will not always be met.

Anal Stage (1–3). At the anal stage, children have their first opportunity to exhibit control and gain independence. While being toilet-trained, infants have the opportunity to release or withhold—their first control. Consequently, personality patterns become further molded at this stage of development. For example, an *anal explosive* personality, defined by being messy and disorganized, may begin to develop and create a lifelong pattern. Conversely, the more commonly studied *anal retentive* people typically exert great control over their own toileting behaviors early in life and continue as adults to be orderly, controlled, and structured.

Phallic Stage (3–5). The phallic stage is characterized by a major shift in gratification. Beginning sexual urges are the source of great fear. Children at this stage have many difficult tasks to overcome, and often their later problems in life germinate here. In the phallic stage, toddlers develop an attraction to their opposite-sex parent. This strong yet unconscious desire becomes a well of difficulty. Little boys, attracted to their mother, desire her, yet someone much bigger and more powerful—Dad—stands in the way. This challenge, called the *Oedipus complex*, is difficult to resolve. The small and physically weak toddler learns that his mother lacks a penis. The child believes that, if he attempts to take over his mother, his father will remove the child's penis as well, which results in an overwhelming *fear of castration*. The toddler suppresses these issues deep into his unconscious and begins to identify with his father as the safest way to be close to mom. When they become aware of their physical lacking, female toddlers, too, have a great challenge because they develop *penis envy*. This envy, eliciting the *Electra complex*, creates a great desire for the child's father, but her mother stands in the way, so the female toddler learns to identify with her.

Latency Stage (5–puberty). The latency stage, existing until puberty, is characterized by great repression of sexual urges. Children shove sexual energy deep into their unconscious minds and focus more on developing healthy same-sex relationships. Friendships become their main source of enjoyment and motivation. This stage shows dormant sexual behavior until the all-changing puberty arrives.

Genital Stage (Puberty–death). The genital stage, focused on genital sexual gratification, continues throughout life. Freud believed that sexual relationships with the opposite sex begin at this stage and may lead to commitments such as marriage. Although not considered the most challenging stage of development, the genital stage is often plagued by past repressed experiences. Earlier, unconscious experiences influence choices and behaviors often below a person's awareness. These experiences continue to play out through adulthood.

Goals of Therapy. Freud's view of the mind serves as the basis for the goals of therapy. The structure and conflict that occur through the inner workings of the id, ego, and superego create a state of flux and movement. As a person attempts to suppress the primal drives of the id, the ego often struggles to mediate in a world of limited resources, which breeds psychological conflict. The superego, with its demands for moral perfection, also puts great strain on the ego. This strain requires the ego to make decisions in a rational way, while being tugged by two irrational components of the mind. Consequently, the main goal of psychoanalysis is understanding.

Ultimately, the helper's goal is to move a client *through* past repressed memories and mend or remove failing defense mechanisms. Problems of today are rooted in experiences in the past. Helping the client reexperience and move beyond past experiences is key to successful therapy. The unconscious, which houses all the deep thoughts and feelings, continues to be a person's greatest motivation of behavior. Inherent in the structure of the mind, the unconscious is the part about which the least is known. Consequently, much of the goal of therapy is to bring the unconscious forward; uncovering what is hidden becomes a paramount component of successful therapy. If therapy is successful, symptoms will naturally disappear.

Techniques. What would Freud do? Well, of course, movies paint the standard, nearly inevitable picture of a client sprawled upon an antique fainting couch deep in thought speaking fluidly about mom and dad. This scenario is not inevitable, but a similar process is often a component of psychoanalysis. Because the goal of therapy is to make the unconscious conscious, psychoanalytic therapists attempt to remove distractions and resistance, allowing the client to *free-associate*. This technique helps bring the depths of the unconscious forward. In addition, Freud utilized *dream analysis* because it was, in his words, the "royal road to the unconscious." Finally, *interpretation* and *analysis of transference* (in which the client projects feelings through the therapist) further serve to bring the depths of the unconscious forward. These crucial techniques require that the therapist know when to interpret the client's feelings appropriately. This interpretation helps the client understand how current behavior relates to past conflicts and unconscious struggles (Corey, 2004; 2012).

Although often criticized for being a long-term therapy, psychoanalysis attempts to make long-term changes in clients. The integration of the mind and self-awareness are both dynamic and worthy pursuits for moving the client. The techniques mentioned here allow both the therapist and the client to see deep into the unconscious, which helps to explain the client's current feelings, thoughts, and behaviors. As the client's understanding occurs, the therapist helps the client move forward, which contributes to long-term, meaningful change.

Freud and Diversity. Traditional psychoanalytic therapy is often criticized for not being applicable to diverse clients and, at the extreme, "irrelevant" (Ivey, D'Andrea, Ivey, & Simek-Morgan, 2002, p. 125). At the same time, it is typically acknowledged that Freud's thoughts were developed in a time very different from contemporary counseling and psychotherapy. Consequently, gender bias is often offered as a critique of Freud, and traditional psychoanalytic therapists viewed gay, lesbian, and bisexual clients as dysfunctional. However, most psychoanalytic therapists today have broadened the traditional approach to be applicable to diverse populations. Contemporary theories that developed from psychoanalytic theory, such as *objection relations theory* (eg., Klein, 1975), are often considered to be more generalizable to diverse populations. If traditional psychoanalytic approach becomes your chosen theoretical orientation, it is advised you look closely at how to utilize this approach best when working with diverse clients.

Freud and the Intentional Theory Selection Model. Obviously, Freud lived long before the ITS model. In this historical highlight, Freud had presented *the* theory of psychotherapy. During the conception of Freud's work, no theories of helping competed with it. Other theories in existence at the time focused primarily on spiritual and biological issues, not on psychological ones. So how would Freud's conceptualization look? At the base was his philosophy of life, which caused him to view humans as deterministic and pleasure seeking. His school of thought was his own psychodynamic school, and his theoretical orientation was his own psychoanalytic theory. Through his own research, Freud developed his goals and techniques based on his own philosophy. He wanted to help his clients through techniques, such as *free association* and *dream analysis*, to understand how their deterministic nature and innate pleasure-seeking behaviors caused their presenting problems. Figure 4.1 shows the ITS model as it applies to Freud's theory.

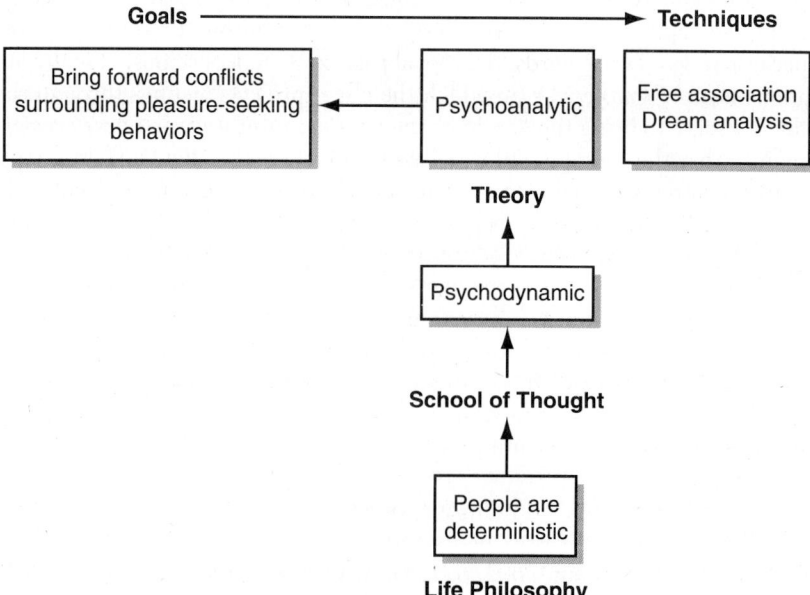

FIGURE 4.1 A Psychoanalytic ITS Model

Analytical Theory

A one-time student, mentee, and "adopted son" of Freud, Carl G. Jung offered an intuitively developed, creative, and dynamic view of the psyche and human development called *analytical theory*. Around midlife, Jung had a near psychological breakdown—leaving his work and much of his life behind. Although he is described as nearly going mad, he emerged from this time with a greater development of his theory, which, following his psychic change, truly only barely resembled Freud's and had many distinctive differences.

Life Philosophy. Jung believed that people are holistic individuals connected at an ancestral level. He agreed with Freud that people possess physical drives. However, he believed that one's main life pursuit was to move intentionally toward *individuation*, which is a force that pushes us toward wholeness and helps *the self* to emerge. Although not historically designated as an existentialist, Jung felt that people longed for life meaning, and he identified humans as having a highly spiritual dimension.

Jung viewed humans positively. He did acknowledge that people's past influenced who they were. However, he took a less deterministic view of life that assumed people actively moved toward their potential. Consequently, Jung deemed that development occurs throughout the life span and believed that actualization occurs later in life.

Jung offered a unique perspective of personality and is credited with coining the term *psyche*. In Jung's view, the psyche is composed of three major systems: the ego; the personal unconscious; and the ancestral, collective unconscious. The *ego*—people's current thoughts, feelings, and reflections—is easy to access and contains their current experiences. Those emotions that people experience at the present time and the information that they are currently absorbing are housed in the ego and are accessible and present. The *personal unconscious* houses those memories and thoughts that are filed away, accessible but more difficult to reach. If you imagine the face of your fourth-grade teacher, likely you accessed your personal unconscious. The teacher's face was likely accessible but was not at first present in your ego. At the deepest level and very difficult to access is the *collective unconscious*. Through the study of myths, languages, and art, Jung realized that all cultures, from the most primitive to the most civilized, have common themes and stories. He found strong connections between cultures and identified a deeper, ancestral level to our psyche. Deep within this ancestral level, people contain *archetypes*, which are basic icons that build their personality. For example, all people contain *shadow, the wise one, healer, anima* (our female side), *animus* (our male side), and *hero* images. When people have life experiences, they build upon these archetypes, which formulate their personality. These archetypes serve as building blocks for categorizing and organizing experiences, ultimately making people who they are.

These archetypes, which are typically hidden from one's awareness, are expressed in dreams, religions, myths, and cultural symbols. For example, take a Disney cartoon, a contemporary film, or any fable and decide who (or what) represents the hero and the shadow. Jung believed that these symbols of the collective unconscious could be found from the most contemporary of societies to the most primitive, isolated tribes.

Human connection serves to bind all people in some way while still allowing individual personality to emerge.

Jung, like Freud, believed that people are motivated by *libidinal energy*. Later, however, Jung came to oppose Freud's sexual and aggressive understanding of libido and perceive libido instead as creative life energy with a biological basis. This energy—moving back and forth, never lost or created, but placed in various areas of one's psyche—was in constant movement. For example, people could place all of their energy in their creative, aggressive shadow side. Embracing their "evilness," people could entertain a life in which they saw only negative in others and enjoyed controlling others though aggression. However, people could have energy fixated in their hero side, so that they were always looking for the hidden good in others while trying to care for them. Consequently, where people focus their libido drives their behavior and emotions.

Goals of Therapy. For Jung, a main goal of therapy is the integration of the psyche. Because he believed that people have a set and limited amount of psyche energy, they must find balance in their psychological world and intentionally help their *self* to emerge. This emerging self enables people ultimately to be full-functioning individuals. The main goal of counseling is *individuation*, or the integration of the conscious and unconscious systems through insight, personality transformation, and even education (Kaufmann, 1979).

This individuation and emerging of the self make up a lifelong, intentional journey. Unlike Freud, Jung believed that midlife is the first time an individual could begin to have integration, and he focused on the emerging of the psyche instead of the causes. As people grow, mature, and move toward individuation, they acknowledge and embrace all parts of themselves—the hero, anima, animus, healer, and even shadow. Without this intention and integration, the true self could never emerge. Regarding individuation, Jung (1991) states:

> So although the objective psyche can only be conceived as a universal and uniform datum, which means that all men share the same primary, psychic condition, this objective psyche must nevertheless individuate itself if it is to become actualized for there is no other way in which it could express itself except through the individual human being. (p. 179)

Techniques. Jung did whatever it took for the client to gain insight. He was highly creative in therapy and believed in doing whatever was necessary for healing (e.g., Green, 2008; McClary, 2007). First and foremost, however, Jung believed the analyst and client should have a warm relationship, which is the foundation of quality therapy. Egalitarian, respectful relationships are the core to therapy. He believed that only through these relationships would clients have the comfort to share their stories and have the room to experience catharsis. Although Jung was known to sing, pray, dance, utilize art, and even examine astrological charts, he is most known for two techniques—*dream analysis* and *archetypal analysis*.

Jung believed that dreams ultimately help people see the deepest layer of their unconscious. Through a process of self-understanding, people can strive, grow, and enhance. If you, as a helper, espouse a Jungian paradigm, you understand that clients reach for individuation and health as they gain a greater understanding of their psyche and that this understanding can be achieved best through archetypal analysis.

Analysis helps to bring insight, which is the key to change. For example, we had a client in her early forties who was struggling with assertiveness and presenting with marital difficulties. She shared the following dream:

> I was fighting with my husband, and he looked like me. I was trying to pull him in, almost into me. Not like I was going to eat him but . . . well, it sounds weird, because at the same time I was yelling at him and pushing him away, I was trying to hug him. He kept saying, "Don't push me away, you need me." I didn't know what to do. I never really felt anger in the dream, but just fear or even guilt. I felt like it was wrong for me to hold on to him.

The client wisely believed the dream was a commentary on her marriage. She did push her husband away and yet wanted to draw nearer to him. To an analytic helper, however, the dream was something more individual, a commentary on the client. As a midlife individual, her goals were integration and individuation. Her husband represented her animus—the male part of herself. Her goal of being assertive was hindered by the guilt and fear of embracing her more masculine (animus) side. The dream was telling her "you need" to integrate your animus and anima. Once she understood the dream, the client was much more able to be assertive without feeling guilt.

Analytic Psychology and Diversity. Carl Jung's work has a variety of thoughts regarding how to apply his work best to diverse clients. His approach emerged from looking at the commonalities of all people across cultures. Consequently, analytic therapists value the cultural context of all clients, highlighting this as an effective approach across cultures. Therapy commonly looks at dreams and spiritual aspects, and assumes basic commonalities of all people, which could challenge some clients' belief systems. Analytical therapies believe in being creative and meeting clients where they come from, however, and are thus thought to be applicable to a wide range of clients.

Individual Psychology

Another prodigy of Freud, Alfred Adler, also believed humans were motivated by a few very basic needs. However, Adler, especially later, had differing views on concepts such as the ego and psychopathology (Ansbacher, 1985; Maniacci, 2007). Adler did believe parental relationships are important; however, the major need and focus of development are centered on socialization.

Life Philosophy. *Gemeinschaftsgefühl*, typically translated as "social interest," is the core tenet of individual psychology. Adler became disenchanted with Freud's deterministic view that people are primarily sexual beings. Like Freud, Adler believed that one's primary personality is constructed and set at an early age. Consequently, he focused great energy on understanding early life development and the role one plays in the family. Parenting style, sibling rivalry, and even childhood illness write the roles one will continue to play later in life. Parents who give too much, too little, or the wrong type of support may risk their child's ability ultimately to become a socially mature and useful person.

As reflected in the title of Adler's approach, people are holistic individuals (*indiviuum* is Latin for "individual" or "whole"). A major contrast to the reductionism that Freud endorsed, this approach looks at the various components that make people human. Adler's concern was the entirety and completeness of the person.

People are also *teological* (goal-directed) creatures. All of one's actions, even the smallest, seemingly random action, serve a purpose and can be understood when the goal is discovered. Adler believed that people have free will, free choice, and a *creative power* to choose their behaviors; consequently, they can choose new goals and behaviors. Unknown to most, each individual has a personal *fictional finalism*, her driving and unattainable goal. Our unattainable fictional finalism serves as all we strive to become. All people develop their own view of what they attempt to reach. People may have goals of being perfect, good, godlike, the perfect father, the funniest person, and so on. These goals may guide their behavior but are immeasurable and ultimately unobtainable. For example, a boy may strive to be the perfect son. His behaviors along the way help him, as he views it, to make this happen. Although this goal is immeasurable, striving to attain it drives his everyday behaviors.

As people strive to meet their life goals, they commonly develop smaller goals along the way to reaching their fictional finalism. However, these smaller goals may not always be effective in other areas of their life. These *mistaken goals* lead people to make decisions that have emotional consequences. For example, if a boy is striving to become the perfect son, he may make the assumption that this goal requires him always to give of himself and not to meet his personal needs. Consequently, at the extreme, this goal will not work to bring him happiness. If he meets every situation believing that he must give, he may ultimately become drained and even resentful of others.

Adler believed innate to being born is a feeling of *inferiority*. People's natural beginning state is one where they feel "less than." However, this state is not a weakness or abnormality and serves truly to be a powerful motivation of human behavior. Due to their beginning stance, people strive to achieve superiority. This motivates them to achieve as they attempt to compensate for this feeling. If people do not develop ways to accomplish this, they run the risk of developing an *inferiority complex*, which includes a pervasive feeling that one is less than others. An additional risk is the acquisition of a *superiority complex*: an attempt to overcompensate for one's own inferiority feelings with grandiose opinions of one's talents and success (Adler, Ansbacher, & Ansbacher, 1989).

In pursuit of the ultimate personal goal, Adler identified various *styles of life*, influenced by early experiences to help people along their goal-oriented journey. According to Adler, as social beings, people have several *life tasks* to accomplish. These tasks include *love, friendship, occupation, family*, and *spirituality*. Each of these tasks has unique social challenges. In this pursuit, the various styles of life drive how people are or are not successful in achieving them. The styles of life serve as the "spectacles" through which the person perceives her own life (Mosak, 1979, p. 44). As part of people's styles of life, they lean toward a personality type. *Dominant-type* people lack social interest and often hurt themselves or others. Common *getting-type* people expect others to meet their needs and frequently become dependent upon others. *Avoiding-type* people minimize contact with others and the world, ultimately avoiding failure and success. These three types of individuals offer little to others, consistently struggle with problem solving, and have limited social interest. The fourth, and most healthy, style of life is the *socially useful type*. These individuals are able to accomplish the basic tasks of life while being socially minded. They typically contribute to the elevation of the human condition and society in general.

Goals of Therapy. Adler believed that the bulk of an individual's personality is established in the early years of life. As creative individuals, however, people do have the ability to change. Through insight, their perceptions can change, which in turn creates personal and behavioral change. Because people are social creatures, increasing the social interest of clients is the ultimate goal of therapy.

In the process of change, it is often important to examine the *private logic* of the individual. These personal cognitive and emotional abilities are designed to help each person to achieve life goals. However, disruptive private logic, inferiority/superiority complexes, and mistaken goals all contribute to daily discouragement. Consequently, the goal of therapy is change—to reconfigure private logic, to gain healthy goals, and to accomplish life tasks in socially useful ways.

Techniques. Adlerian therapists first establish a therapeutic alliance: a relationship centered on warmth and collaboration. After establishing rapport, which is a necessary step for an Adlerian helper, a lifestyle assessment is required. Learning the client's family constellation, including birth order, early recollections, private logic, and fictional finalism, is key to client change. Lifestyle assessment is the key to the therapeutic process because it assists the helper in learning about the client and later providing the client with insight and interventions.

The client's *constellation* represents the roles played within the family. These roles affect who the client is today. Understanding how people view their developmental years tells the helper who they really are today. Adlerians also focus on gathering *early recollections*, a person's early memories. These recollections tell the helper much about the client's style of life and goals. The Adlerian helper believes that the important issue is not the reality and objectivity of early recollections but rather the client's subjective meaning that is revealed in early recollections. The roles clients play in their early recollections will likely continue to be played in their contemporary lives. For example, here are three early recollections from a client named Anton: First, when Anton was four, his kitten disappeared, never to return. Second, when he was five, a neighbor child whom he feared stole his shoes. Third, when he was seven, his brother broke his favorite toy, a Star Wars Chewbacca doll. You likely see a theme. What do you think these early recollections say about Anton today? The recollections of the past he shares about himself speak to who he is today. The Adlerian therapist would look at these early recollections and attempt to find patterns or themes. In this case, the therapist might see that Anton felt hurt and loss in each of these situations; he felt like others were taking away what was then important to him. Through an Adlerian perspective, this would suggest that today, as an adult, he feels as though others take from him unfairly.

First, the Adlerian helper establishes rapport. Then he or she conducts a thorough assessment that includes gaining an understanding of the client's lifestyle, early recollections, birth order, family constellation, goals, and private logic. Beyond these, Adlerians present many pragmatic techniques, such as *acting as if*, *pushing the button*, *paradoxical interventions*, and *catching oneself*, that help clients to gain insight and make behavioral changes (these are defined in detail elsewhere; see e.g., Mosak, 1985; Murdock, 2009).

Individual Psychology and Diversity. Although Adler's approach is called *individual psychology*, Adler and his contemporaries acknowledged the importance of social context for clients (Arciniega & Newlon, 1999) and understood the necessity to understand clients from the client's own cultural background. It is possible that the focus on *self* could be a challenge in working with clients who come from a collectivist culture. The family is considered so important in bringing about understanding and change, and clients from cultures that feel psychological challenges bring shame or embarrassment on the family may be reluctant to provide open dialogue surrounding family issues. However, several have proposed that, when done correctly, the Adlerian approach has few limitations in multicultural settings (Corey, 2012) and is often complimented as a diverse-friendly approach. Adler may be considered the first *feminist* in the history of psychotherapy because he believed men and women should be treated equally. His belief that all individuals should be treated equally was evidenced in counseling sessions during which equalitarian relationships were promoted.

BEHAVIORAL SCHOOL OF THOUGHT

The behavioral approach takes a much different look at human behavior: Humans are shaped and determined by sociocultural conditioning. This paradigm is basically deterministic because all behaviors are believed to be a product of learning through conditioning and reinforcement. Effective as well as ineffective behaviors are learned and typically are the result of learned or expected consequences. True, traditional behaviorists take a scientific, empirical approach and primarily focus on tangible behaviors, goals, and techniques.

Traditional behavioral thinking has many contemporary variations. The process of therapy still focuses on behavioral aspects of clients, but it does not ignore the need for emotional expression and a warm therapeutic relationship. For the purpose of example, only behavioral therapy will be introduced here because this approach outlines the original philosophy of the behavioral school of thought.

Behavioral Therapy

B. F. Skinner (1976) in *Walden Two* describes a utopian society where behavioral techniques are utilized to reduce the need for individual morality and make the need for personal value unnecessary. This revolutionary, controversial writing made practical the value of behavioral therapy. While the concept of utopian societies may have little to do with today's counseling and psychotherapy, the work of B. F. Skinner does.

Life Philosophy. Nearly every day, professionals and laypersons use techniques from behavioral therapy. Spanking, speeding tickets, gambling casinos, and even employee-of-the-month programs are all the results of several key behavioral theories. Behavioral therapists believe that people's behaviors are products of their environment and that their actions are the results of what happens to them. Behaviorists see people as genetic creatures. However, as empiricists, behaviorists believe people should examine only that which can be observed and measured. If something cannot be tasted, touched, felt, heard, or seen, it is not essential to therapy. Consequently, more value is placed on the present than on past experiences. Behaviorists are known for their adherence to the scientific method and objective approach to psychotherapy. An additional life view of the behaviorists is that we are all basically *hedonistic*—pleasure seeking. People seek reward and pleasure while avoiding punishment and pain.

What causes emotional and behavioral problems in life? Learning—the process that creates healthy emotions and behaviors—also creates problems. Because *all* behavior is reinforced through the process of learning, both positive and negative behaviors and their respective consequences are learned. Each person is unique, and each has a unique learning history. The rewards people experience and the consequences (both good and bad) they endure cause their behaviors.

Traditional behavioral approaches have three major theoretical underpinnings that describe human behavior: *classical conditioning*, *operant conditioning*, and *social learning theory*.

Classical Conditioning. Early in the twentieth century, while studying the digestive systems of dogs, Ivan Pavlov made an interesting discovery. He found that he could ring a bell and dogs would drool. His discovery forms the basis of many behavioral techniques and describes many basic human behaviors.

Pavlov showed that a stimulus that should not cause an automatic reaction could be made to do so. Pavlov rang his bell and gave his dogs food powder. What did they do? Salivate. He rang his bell again, gave the powder, and what did his dogs do? Salivate. Yet again he rang his bell and gave the powder. What did the dogs do? You are correct. They salivated. Then he again rang his bell without giving the dogs the powder. What did the dogs do? Yes, again, they salivated. The powder was an *unconditioned stimulus*, meaning it caused an automatic reaction—in this case, drooling—the *unconditioned response*. When a neutral stimulus, like the bell, is repeatedly paired with an unconditioned stimulus, like the powder, the bell becomes a conditioned *stimulus* that can elicit a response—the *conditioned response*—on its own. Thus, learning occurs.

Operant Conditioning. Although classical conditioning seemed to explain many behaviors, others (e.g., Bandura, 1969; Skinner, 1971) believed that there was more to learning. All behaviors have consequences, such as rewards and punishments, that cause behavior. For example, if you make fun of someone's hair, that person may choose to kick you; pain is your consequence, and you will likely no longer make fun. If teachers want to increase the amount of questions their students pose in classes, they might give a dollar to each student after he or she asked a question. An educated bet says that this practice would increase questions and class participation. *Operant conditioning* explains that every behavior is either promoted or not promoted by what follows.

Social Learning Theory. Human behavior is vastly complicated. What we do or don't do is often beyond our own comprehension. For example, ask yourself these questions: "Have you ever run your car over a cliff? If not, why? Have you received positive rewards, like money, for not going over a cliff? Then how did you learn not to?" Social learning theory explains that people also learn vicariously by watching others (Bandura, 1969). If you see a person get punished with a parking ticket for illegal parking, you can learn vicariously from that person's mistake. Behavioral therapists believe we can learn from observing the behaviors of others.

Goals of Therapy. In many ways, the goals of behavioral therapy are the most straightforward of the contemporary psychotherapy approaches. Behavioral therapists spend their time with clients addressing specific behaviors that help their clients learn to behave differently (e.g., Daly, Creed, Xanthopoulos, & Brown, 2007; Pagoto, Bodenlos, Schneider, Olendzki, & Spates, 2008; Weiskeop, Richdale, & Matthews, 2005). In this process, clients are often empowered to set specific goals that are relevant to them and their current presenting problem.

For therapy to be effective, data must be collected, goals must be set, and relevant interventions must be initiated. As an objective approach, behavioral therapy examines outcomes and strives to initiate assessments based on these interventions. The goals of therapy include helping clients to change their environment, because environment is truly the cause of all behaviors, and reinforcing new, more effective behaviors.

Techniques. Behavioral therapists utilize many techniques that are based primarily on classical conditioning, operant conditioning, and social learning theory. Techniques focus on changing the environment and behavioral consequences because all behaviors are fundamentally based on learning. The tool belt of a behavioral therapist is full and includes tools such as education, reinforcement scheduling, modeling, systematic desensitization, relaxation techniques, assertiveness and skills training, charting, contracts, aversion therapy, satiation, self-monitoring, and homework assignments (Corey, 2012; Day, 2004; Gilliland & James, 1998; Ivey, Ivey, D'Andrea, & Simek-Downing, 2007). Behaviorists have been highly creative and have given the helping professions many tools to use. One example is the *token economy*. This intervention is based on giving small rewards for positive behaviors that can later be traded in for larger awards. Behaviorists have also given us *aversion therapy*, based on classical conditioning. A behavior can be limited by pairing it with something that is not enjoyable. For example, if you want to quit biting your nails, a helping professional might suggest that you put extremely hot pepper seeds under your nails. Soon nail biting will be associated with pain, and you will learn a new behavior: stop biting your nails.

Behaviorism and Diversity. The behaviorist approach is often considered applicable to all clients. The foundations of therapy and the techniques and evidence to prove their effectiveness go beyond cultural boundaries. Learning and behavior are universal across cultures and demographic characteristics, including age. Consequently, behaviorism works well with diverse populations (Corey, 2012). This makes it easy for counselors and psychotherapists to avoid the pitfalls that can happen when their values have an impact on therapeutic endeavors.

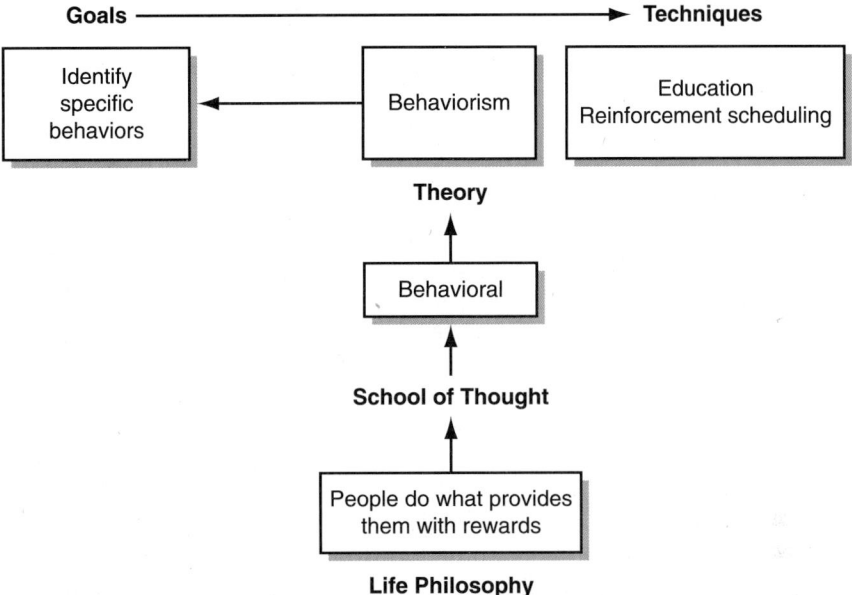

FIGURE 4.2 Jim's ITS Model

A Behaviorist School Counselor and the Intentional Theory Selection Model. Jim, a graduating therapist and school counselor, believed, as do most behaviorists, that the key to changing a child's behavior is identifying target behaviors and changing reinforcements that perpetuate these behaviors. Jim commonly works with students whom teachers have identified as acting out. He has found that certain students who disturb the classroom environment often get attention only when they act out. Consequently, Jim focuses on educating teachers about behavioral phenomena and assists them in creating reinforcement schedules that reward students when they are on task and performing well in the classroom. Jim's ITS model might look like Figure 4.2.

HUMANISTIC SCHOOL OF THOUGHT

The core belief of the humanistic school is that humans have a basic inclination to become *fully functioning*, to develop and grow psychologically. Individuals are viewed in a positive manner, and the context of therapy is often focused on the affective world of the client, moving toward self-actualization, gaining trust, achieving spontaneity, and focusing on the human condition. Humanistic approaches take a phenomenological, here-and-now approach. The relationship between the client and therapist is thought to be fundamental to successful therapy and helping clients achieve their potential. The most common humanistic approaches are *person-centered, existential,* and *Gestalt*.

Person-Centered

The focus of the person-centered approach (also referred to as the Rogerian, client-centered, or nondirective approach) is truly inherent in the theory's title. The person-centered approach typifies the humanistic approach and focuses on he client and the world of the client as the center of therapeutic change.

Life Philosophy. The true person-centered helper views the world and human nature as positive. People, left to their own volition, continually strive to reach their potential (Rogers, 1961). A fundamental belief is that humans strive toward *self-actualization* in a process of growth. Self-actualization, the process of moving toward one's greatest potential, is never achieved but is a continuous process. This actualization requires one to grow and gain experience constantly.

Person-centered helpers believe everyone is unique and everyone has a unique worldview. Consequently, clients should be understood in a *phenomenological* approach, which requires the therapist to attempt to see the world as clients see it. Although often hard to remember as a helper, the clients' emotions and actions make sense given the way they view the world. Carl Rogers (1995), often considered the father of humanistic therapy, stated that it is important "to open one's spirit to what is going on *now*, and to discover in that present process whatever structure it appears to have" (p. 189). Rogers also believed that life and therapy are characterized by a subjective reality and should be immersed in the here and now. Each moment is unique, and people are defined not by their past but by who they are in the moment.

Person-centered helpers believe that clients ultimately know themselves better than therapists could ever know them. Clients are experts on their own lives. Consequently, person-centered helpers may offer little advice and few directives. They might be directive about the process of therapy, but they allow their clients to make their own choices. This approach serves many purposes, including empowering the client. The value of this stance is highlighted in this trite but concrete example. Imagine you could go to a therapist and ask what you should wear for a big interview; the answer given to you is "the red power tie." If you get the job, you might think it had more to do with the helper's choices than with your abilities. In contrast, if you did not get the job, you might be angry with the helper and feel you were led astray. A person-centered helper should help you find what you want and what ultimately works for you. You are assisted in the process of finding your own answers, which empowers you beyond one specific situation.

Goals of Therapy. The major goal of therapy is ultimately to help the individual continue toward self-actualization. At times, however, life situations or the individual's perceptions may hinder growth. The road to actualization can become blocked, and therapy is about removing these blocks. People have a natural tendency to move forward to reach their greatest potential, and they can surpass difficulties only through removing these blocks.

Does this mean people must have large problems to be in therapy? No. Something will always be in the way of reaching their complete potential. Therapy can focus on prevention of struggles at predictable life transitions or simply on helping someone become "more." Therapy is actually most effective for those who are relatively healthy (Yalom, 1995) because they have the energy, insight, and potential to learn and consequently to grow psychologically.

A common block people often face is a distorted view of self (Gilliland & James, 1998). Through the process of therapy, helpers hope their clients can find greater self-understanding and increased congruence between their *ideal self* and their *real self*. This difference between who people want to be and how they perceive themselves can cause great psychological turmoil and is a major roadblock to people living to their greatest potential. If a workshop attendee gives speakers negative feedback about their presentation style, the speakers may believe they are "bad public speakers," which may not be true. They may be great public speakers but view themselves as less skilled based on this limited information. This view creates anxiety; the job of the counselor is not to "directly reduce anxiety" (Hazler, 2003, p. 166) but to increase congruence between the ideal and real self. Consequently, a healthier self-concept is often the result of effective therapy.

Techniques. People are individuals with different needs and wants. Therapy is immersed in phenomenology and the here and now. Consequently, directives and typical techniques are not common in the person-centered approach. In contrast, the cornerstone of the person-centered approach is the therapeutic relationship. *Genuineness*, the ability to be *nonjudgmental*, and *empathy* are the keys to therapy and the therapeutic alliance. These three core conditions of therapy are *necessary* and *sufficient* for change to occur (Rogers, 1957).

Genuineness, or the ability to be authentic, requires helper transparency. Therapists must be aware of their own feelings and allow this awareness to be part of the relationship. Clients know when therapists are being dishonest, so developing facades only harms the therapeutic relationship. Being truly authentic is difficult, however; it requires self-knowledge and understanding, and it takes the ability to know and share one's self. These requirements challenge helpers in cognitive and emotional dimensions and also force them to serve with congruence, being honest in both words and actions: "Congruence is the stream upon which accurate and therapeutic communication travel" (Quinn, 2008, p. 461). This *congruence* challenges us as helpers because it requires us to use ourselves as a therapeutic tool and reveal ourselves as individuals.

Being nonjudgmental, or offering *unconditional positive regard*, requires helpers to completely and wholly accept their clients (Rogers, 1957, 1995). Therapists must not put conditions on therapeutic relationships in order for an environment of trust and acceptance to occur. They do not have to accept all that their clients do, but they must accept clients at the core for being human. To be truly effective, therapists must accept clients in their entirety.

For therapy to be successful, therapists must convey *empathy* to their clients. Empathy is, first, the ability to see the world through the eyes of another and, second, the ability to convey this insight. This empathy requires that therapists take a phenomenological approach and truly listen to the affective world of their clients. Person-centered therapy requires such basic truly powerful skills such as the ability to reflect the client's narrative, to listen, and to paraphrase it all—all while producing rapport. As a helper, understanding and having insight are important. To help clients move toward their potential, however, therapists must have the ability to share this insight with clients—to show them that they see their joys and struggles.

Being Person-Centered in a Diverse World. With a phenomenological approach, it is hard to find a critique of a person-centered perspective from a multicultural context because the phenomenological approach prompts understanding clients from their cultures. Within the literature, however, a few potential limitations have been noted. One, the focus on the individual may have a negative impact for clients who come from collectivist cultures (Corey, 2012; Murdock 2012). Many clients, especially those from cultures who believe therapy may be an embarrassment to their family, come to therapy as a last resort. Some clients from culturally diverse backgrounds will expect therapy to be directive (Corey, 2012), and an approach that does not use such techniques with these clients may be difficult for them to accept. However, the person-centered approach has also been highlighted as being open to diversity, striving toward understanding diverse cultures, and emphasizing the client's values as paramount to the therapy. The goal of the therapist is to truly understand clients from their worldview and their culture, and thus the person-centered approach has great promise in work with clients from all races, ethnicities, religions, orientations, socioeconomic statuses, and abilities.

Existential

Why are we here? What happens when we die? What is our purpose? How can we live a meaningful life? These questions lie at the core of the existential approach. The fundamental questions of existence are core to people's successes and challenges in life.

Life Philosophy. Often known as philosophical helpers, existentialists have woven their fabric into the tapestry of humanism. Existentialists are often misperceived as pessimistic because they deal with fundamental issues such as death, isolation, and anxiety and with questions of existence. They help clients deal with the fundamental and basic conditions of being human. For example, existentialists view life as ultimately meaningless (Yalom, 1995). Some people may see this view as discouraging or sad; in the existential paradigm, however, it offers people an opportunity to create their own life meaning and pursue their own life purpose. This belief allows people to make their life personal and to tailor their life's work to who they are.

Existentialists believe that anxieties and worries are ultimately consequences of basic and core conditions of life. People's most basic emotions stem from acknowledging the realities of life. For example, the fact that one will ultimately die creates great psychological stress. People question what death is like and what happens following death, and they may even imagine the world without them. This arena of the unknown creates angst. People want to have answers to these difficult questions but often do not. Knowing that they will die reminds people that they are limited in the time they have to accomplish their goals. Death is a constant reminder that in order to do all they want, or to say all they want, people are working with an unknown timeframe.

Existentialists also acknowledge that people have complete freedom within their capabilities. This freedom often frightens people, however, so they often pretend not to have it. For example, you might often like to sleep in. However, you *feel* you must go to work as opposed to sleeping in. You do not actually have to go because you have the freedom to do what you want. However, knowing that you are completely free can be scary. This realization challenges people's view of the securities they have.

People struggle with knowing that they are responsible for their own lives, and they often fight accepting responsibility and look to blame others for the consequences of not accepting responsibility. If people do not accept that they are the makers of their own situations, they run the risk of not taking control of their own lives.

Several authors (e.g., Corey, 2004) consider existential psychotherapy to be more of a philosophical approach than a unique humanist approach. Existentialism serves as a way to view clients but is not a completely unique approach. Although existentialism has common identified tenets (Halbur, 2000), individual existentialists themselves are unique. Each individual is understood as unique, so it makes sense that there are as many existential approaches as there are existentialists.

Existential psychotherapy does not replace but builds upon humanism. Consequently, it is also present-focused, phenomenological, and holistic; believes in the uniqueness of others; and attempts to help others continue toward self-actualization. Rogers (1995) writes, "It is this tendency toward existential living which appears to me very evident in people who are involved in the process of the good life" (p. 189). He believed that a component of actualization is to live in an existential way.

Goals of Therapy. Awareness is a major goal in existential psychotherapy (Corey, 2004; Yalom, 1980). Like person-centered therapy, existential psychotherapy focuses on moving forward and continuing toward actualization. However, existentialists also believe that their duty is to facilitate a process through which clients can confront conflicts and ultimately issues of existence, meaning, and what being human means (Hansen, Rossberg, & Cramer, 1993; Yalom, 1980). More specifically, this goal includes awareness of the possibilities available, one's freedom to choose, responsibility for one's choices, and barriers to freedom.

Another major goal in existential therapy is acceptance of the core conditions of being human. Helping clients to acknowledge their freedom and use it wisely is important. Accepting one's personal freedom is a much more difficult task than merely being aware. Acceptance of responsibility is also key. Many clients have said, "I know I can do it," yet they do not follow through. To be active and to take control of one's self and one's life is important. As a helper, you can serve to empower clients to make personal choices and to have the courage to follow through.

An additional and paramount goal of therapy is to help people find or create meaning in their behavior, their lives, and even their suffering (Frankl, 1967;

Kottler & Brown, 1992). Accepting that life is meaningless is difficult, especially if people do not then take the next step to rediscover or create meaning in their lives. The existential helper assists clients in discovering or rediscovering meaning in their lives.

Techniques. As was discussed in the person-centered approach, the helping relationship is necessary, and for the most part sufficient, for effective psychotherapy. This relationship continues to require the therapist's acceptance, authenticity, and empathy. The therapist's task is to enter the client's world and understand the client's unique worldview (Corey, 2004; Kottler & Brown, 1992). The counselor's role is also to be present as clients confront their concerns, rather than acting as a problem solver (Corey, 2004), while helping clients accept responsibility for their own choices (Ivey et al., 1987). In general, however, existential counseling is not technique-oriented; it is relationship-focused and may utilize techniques from other supporting counseling approaches. Existential shock therapy, client disclosure, therapist disclosure, acceptance of responsibility, paradoxical intention, and existential discourse (Becker, 2006; Frankl, 1973; May 1983; Yalom, 1980, Yalom, 2002) have all been suggested as "techniques" utilized in existential approaches. Although they are not traditional techniques and interventions common to other therapeutic approaches, these tools and general counselor characteristics are utilized to help promote client change.

Existentialism and Diversity. Existentialism as an overall approach is often thought to be highly effective with a diverse clientele. Similar to previously addressed theories, however, the focus on the individual may challenge those from collectivist cultures because they may struggle with feeling completely understood. As a phenomenological approach, however, existentialism focuses on the individual's values, beliefs, and cultures. Albert Camus states, "[S]eeking what is true is not seeking what is desirable." Ultimately existential therapists seek to understand what clients believe is their own reality. Thus, existential therapists strive to understand the client; his or her choices, feelings, and behaviors; and the way meaning is constructed by the client. An effective existentialist would approach a client from a collectivistic culture, or any other culture, by attempting to understand the client from his or her worldview and accepting that as the client's reality.

An Existential Psychotherapist and the Intentional Theory Selection Model. John, a psychotherapist who specializes in addictions, has offered consultation to Kristin, a beginning substance abuse counselor. Kristin stated, "My clients drink, use, and abuse because it is all that fills voids in their lives. Nothing else gives them meaning. . . . It's like it's all they have to live for." Kristin said that she had struggled finding a theory that worked for her and that "people are free to make choices, good or bad." John asked Kristin to identify her goals with clients, and she said, "To help them stop using drugs and alcohol and replace their use with more meaningful experiences." Based on this discussion, John thought her ITS might look something like Figure 4.3.

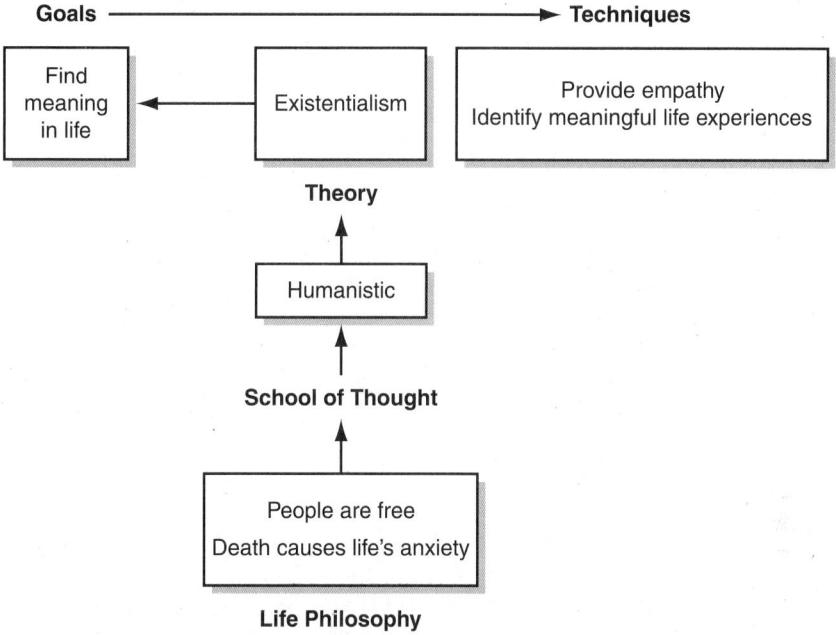

FIGURE 4.3   Kristin's ITS Model

Gestalt

Human experience, behaviors, and reactions are vastly complex. Physically, we are primarily carbon, oxygen, water, and sugar. These ingredients are the components that make up human beings. However, we are more than the sum of our parts—the mantra of Gestalt therapy.

Life Philosophy.   With strong roots in German philosophy and many parallels to the perceptual field of Gestalt psychology, Gestalt therapy is attributed primarily to the work of Fritz Perls (e.g., Perls, 1969a). The term *gestalt* is German meaning "a unified whole" and is the foundation of this humanistic approach.

Gestalt Psychology.   To understand the philosophy of Fritz Perls, you must first understand some basic assumptions of Gestalt psychology. Gestalt psychologists believe that individual components, such as the sugar in cola, have no meaning without their complementary components. Isolated parts are meaningful only when viewed holistically. Humans by nature attempt to bring about gestalts—they attempt to organize data into complete wholes. We even attempt to fill in what is missing in day-to-day experiences. Gestalt psychologists identified several key perceptual tendencies, with the easiest to explain being visual. One is the *principle of closure*. People's nature is to finish experiences that are lacking key details, to make sense of data. People also tend to organize based on the *principle of proximity*. Items that are close together tend to be grouped together. For example, what do you see in the following groupings?

```
O O O            O  O  O            O O O
O O O            O  O  O            O O O
O O O            O  O  O            O O O
```

Most individuals see a square made of circles in the first group, three columns of circles in the second, and three rows of circles in the third. This is due to people's desire to organize and make sense of data. In all three groupings, the same amount of ink was used, but how you organized them changed.

Another common way to organize data is through the *principle of similarity*. People have a strong perceptual tendency to group like objects together. For example, what do you see here?

```
O O O O X X X O O O O O O X X X O O O O
O O O X O O O X O O O O X O O O X O O O
O O X O O O O O X O O X O O O O O X O O
O X O O O O O O O X X O O O O O O O X O
X O O O O O O O O O O O O O O O O O O X
X O O O O O O O O O O O O O O O O O O X
```

Most people do *not* see rows of Os and Xs. Yet that is what is printed. Likely they group the Xs together and observe them as a wavy line.

Sometimes, people organize data in very predictable ways. However, you must remember that each person is an individual and organizes data in different ways. Thus, each person lives in his own phenomenological world. Humans are limited when it comes to how much they can take in and can process. People constantly move their perceptual focus. What they focus on at any one time is called *figure* by Gestalt theorists. What grabs people's greatest attention, focus, or figure is highlighted in the rest of their perceptual field, referred to as *ground*. What do you see here?

```
O X O X
O X O X
O X O X
O X O X
```

Most individuals see one of two things, either rows of Os and Xs or alternating columns of Os and Xs. However, they really cannot see them both at once. People's ability to digest all information at the same time is limited.

Several Gestalt psychology tenets become important in understanding Gestalt therapy. First, people actively attempt to organize and form wholes in their figure-ground field. Second, stimuli can be exchanged from ground to figure based on the phenomenological needs of the individual. Third, the individual's awareness of her surrounding field determines the accuracy of her perception (Perls, 1969a).

Gestalt Therapy. If you have an understanding of the Gestaltist mind, you can start to understand Perls. Perls developed his approach based on the tenets of the psychologists. As a humanist, he believed that people have one inherent goal—*self-actualization*.

In this ongoing process, people sometimes separate and lose their wholeness psychologically (Perls, 1969a). Similar to how they perceive, they can focus emotionally only on the *figure* and often lose site of the background.

Goals of Therapy. The main goal of Gestalt therapy is to bring integration. For people to achieve the goal of integration, it is necessary for them to gain awareness. People begin as whole individuals but at times lose their equilibrium. Helping the client to gain a heightened self-awareness is the key for integration. Through awareness, the client can begin to complete gestalts.

Change requires that clients look at themselves and accept or reject what they will integrate. Consequently, a major goal of therapy is to assist clients in gaining a strong sense of self-responsibility. Only through responsibility can the client begin to integrate.

Techniques. Basically, Perls wanted clients to gain awareness of who they are and who they are becoming. Consequently, in line with other humanists, he immersed himself and his clients in the here and now. The past is relevant because it brings one to today, but it is not the focus of therapy. Because each individual sees the world in a unique way, therapy takes a phenomenological approach.

Perls (1969a) accessed a variety of techniques while believing that the helper should not be tied to technique, even going so far as to say, "A technique is a gimmick . . . and should only be used in the extreme case" (p. 1). However, many (e.g., Ivey, Ivey, D'Andrea, & Simek-Morgan, 2007) think that Perls contributed more to techniques and methodology than he did to theory, and many of these techniques are utilized in various counseling approaches. The following are just a few examples.

Empty Chair. The empty-chair technique is likely Perls's most famous technique. It is utilized to help clients move beyond *unfinished business*—unresolved emotions. The counselor simply directs the client to imagine that someone is in the other chair and encourages the client to have a dialogue with the imagined person. Often, the counselor will instruct the client to move to the other (empty) chair and play the various roles. This powerful technique has proved very effective in working with couples and grief issues (e.g., Greenberg & Malcolm, 2002).

Pronouns. Responsibility is key to effective change. Clients often distance themselves from their own issues by referring to themselves in the third person or by using the word *you* instead of *I* in their narrative. The Gestalt helper encourages clients to use personal pronouns such as *I* and *me* to aid in their personal growth.

Sharing Hunches. The role of the counselor is not interpretation, but sharing hunches is a key technique. The counselor stays focused in the present, and it is important for him or her to notice nonverbal messages. For example, the actions of a client who describes something as sad, while smiling and tapping a foot, likely have clinical significance. Sharing the potential meaning, or even asking the client to do so, can help the client gain greater awareness.

Dream Work. Perls promoted the use of dreams in therapy. However, he was not looking for deep-rooted unconscious thought. Instead of engaging in traditional interpretation, he asked the client to play out specific roles or even to finish conversations begun in the dream.

These are just a few of the techniques available to you as a Gestalt helper. These creative and diverse techniques serve to help the client work through emotional impasses and continue toward self-actualization.

Gestalt and Diversity. Gestalt therapy is a highly interactive and creative approach. Consequently, it shows great promise in working with clients from many cultural backgrounds. However, the techniques employed by Gestalt therapists often invoke strong emotional reactions (Corey, 2012). Therapists of all theories should take caution in using Gestalt techniques with diverse clients and remain mindful of how such directive and interactive techniques may affect clients.

PRAGMATIC SCHOOL OF THOUGHT

In the pragmatic approaches, what people think and want is at the root of their emotional and behavioral lives. Consequently, a change in cognition or a realization of one's needs inevitably causes a change in behaviors and emotions. Dysfunction and maladjustment are primarily problems of faulty or irrational thoughts. Other counseling theory texts call this school of thought *cognitive*. This makes sense because therapy is often focused on learning what people need and want and on understanding how their own thoughts and behaviors influence how successful they are in making this happen. However, we choose to call this school pragmatic because therapists from this school often serve in the role of teacher, offering clients commonsense techniques and helping clients learn how to help themselves.

Cognitive-Behavioral

Daily affirmations, sharing positive messages to yourself in the mirror, and promoting positive self-talk are commonsense techniques that exemplify the cognitive-behavioral approach. What people think about themselves and the world around them directly causes their feelings and behaviors.

Life Philosophy. Cognitive-behavioral therapy (CBT) is a contemporary and favored approach of managed-care plans. Attributed primarily to Aaron Beck (1976, 1991), this approach views emotional and behavioral consequences as the result of inner thoughts and cognitions. People control how they feel by what they think. Typically, people feel that they are sad or happy due to what happens to them. "I won the lottery. I am happy!" "I was late for work. I feel guilty." However, how people *view* their experiences is truly important, not what happens to them.

Luckily, people are creative and highly imaginative, and thus they have the ability to perform self-examination (Corey, 2004; Ivey et al., 1987). The core emphasis of change must center on conscious thought (Hansen et al., 1993). However, simple awareness of one's own thoughts and cognitions is not sufficient for change; people must choose and want to live life differently (Ivey et al., 1987).

People's thoughts determine their emotions, and the meaning they attach to events determines their reactions. Psychological distress (a fancy phrase for "bad feelings") is largely due to one's thought processes (Gilliland & James, 1998; Hansen et al., 1993). People have a natural tendency to develop faulty, ineffective thinking. Therapy can be a powerful tool in positively influencing the lives of clients (e.g., McCloskey, Noblett, Deffenbacher, Gollan, & Coccaro, 2008), and many of its supporting researchers (e.g., Rosselló, Bernal, & Rivera-Medina, 2008) see it as more effective than other therapies when working with specific client issues such as phobias, depressive thinking, issues of esteem, and suicidal ideation.

Goals of Therapy. The ultimate goal of CBT is to teach clients to think about how they think so that they can correct faulty reasoning (Nelson-Jones, 2000). The greater goal is to assist clients in changing systematic, faulty thinking and developing the ability to be their own therapists (Nelson-Jones, 2000). As helpers, we are training clients not to need us and to be independent, autonomous human beings. Some specific goals of CBT include helping clients identify, test, and evaluate beliefs and automatic thoughts so that they may change those that are maladaptive (Corey, 2012).

Techniques. In a cognitive-behavioral environment, therapy is largely psychoeducational, and the emphasis is on developing practical skills for dealing with specific problems (Hansen et al., 1993). Cognitive behaviorists typically work collaboratively with clients and believe that a mutual relationship with strong rapport is important in the process. In contrast to the person-centered approach, empathy, genuineness, and unconditional positive regard are considered *necessary* for change, but alone they are not *sufficient*. A therapeutic alliance is needed for change, but technique is needed as well.

Cognitive behaviorists contribute many techniques to the tool belts of contemporary psychotherapists. However, helpers are also willing to use the techniques from many other approaches—especially those of the behaviorists. For example, the behavioral-modification contracting common in the behavioral approach is often utilized when this technique might help clients gain insight regarding personal cognitions.

Some commonplace techniques used in this approach include skills training; assertiveness training; relaxation techniques; and training in areas such as life skills, social skills, and communication (Corey, 2012; Gilliland & James, 1998; Ivey et al, 2002). Cognitive-behavioral therapy, as a directive, dynamic, and temporal approach, uses any technique that can help clients first to identify automatic thoughts and then to change those that are maladaptive. Other techniques that help in this process include role-play, systematic desensitization, flooding, thought stopping, and cognitive modification.

Cognitive Behavioral Therapy and Diversity. Cognitive behavioral therapy is often cited as being effective in multicultural counseling. Although CBT is often considered an empirically validated approach, some studies show CBT as being less effective with some racially and ethnically diverse clients (e.g., Sue & Sue, 2008). It is important for cognitive behaviorists to understand the culture background (Corey, 2012) of their clients and what potential cognitions are common to their cultures.

Rational Emotive Behavioral Therapy

What type of day have you had? No matter how the day has gone, you likely remember what not-so-good events occurred today. If you do, then you, too, likely fall victim to a natural human tendency: Remembering the worst is easier than remembering the best.

Life Philosophy. Rational emotive behavioral therapy (REBT) views human nature as including innate tendencies toward growth, actualization, and rationality as well as opposing tendencies toward irrationality and dysfunction (Ellis, 1962; Gilliland & James, 1998; Hansen et al., 1993; Nelson-Jones, 2000). This polarization creates tension. Clearly, events, facts, and behaviors play a role in one's daily health. However, one's beliefs about these objective events are more important than the actual events or behaviors (Gilliland & James, 1998; Ivey et al., 1987). Left to their own devices, people tend to move toward irrationality. Consequently, their innate thoughts tend to move in a direction that allows negative thoughts to thrive. Because all people's behaviors and emotions are consequences of their internal selves, they have the capacity to change how they act and feel. However, they must attack their irrational thoughts.

With its initial development in the 1950s by Albert Ellis (1962), REBT maintains that most people learn to think irrationally. Even early interactions with parents influence and exaggerate the innate tendency to think in these irrational ways. Because people are developmental creatures, irrational thoughts become ingrained within their belief system at an early age and surface later in life (Gilliland & James, 1998). Humans are capable of change, however, and do so by changing their thoughts (Nelson-Jones, 2000). For example, here is Duane's experience with Penny: Even typing her name causes him to feel a tinge of anger. In Duane's first year as a professor, he met Penny (named by him). He was in a hurry, a big hurry. He needed to get to campus because he was being observed and evaluated in the classroom by a senior faculty member. With his nervous energy, he decided that he could not succeed without the aid of a cold soda, so he stopped at the local grocery. In front of him in the checkout line was Penny. Remember that Duane is in a hurry. Penny said, "It is a good day to use the change in my purse." So, in order to pay her $8.93, she rummaged through her palatial purse, looking for every last penny (thus, the reason for the name bestowed upon her). Duane was getting angry, very angry. As Penny counted out her last penny, she had only $7.53. At this point, Duane began to personally understand rage when Penny took the next three minutes writing a check for $1.40. He was so angry—but why? He was angry because of two major irrational thoughts. First, he believed, "I might be late for my observation. I will then be fired, go broke, and never have money to buy food again." Second, he believed, "My time is more important than Penny's." These irrational thoughts caused him to arrive on campus (and he did arrive on time) sweating, angry, and anxious. Who was at fault? Duane, not Penny. These typical thought patterns are core to much of our emotional distress. Like Duane in this example, we fundamentally create our own emotional pain.

Goals of Therapy. The primary focus of REBT is to change the way people think because thoughts, rather than events, cause emotional problems (Gilliland & James, 1998; Kottler & Brown, 1992). The main goal of REBT is to reduce self-defeating, irrational thinking (Gilliland & James, 1998).

The goals and process of REBT are often summarized using the *ABC method. A* refers to the "activating event" or "adversity." *B* is the individual's "beliefs about the event," which may be rational and helpful or irrational and maladaptive. *C* refers to the "emotional and behavioral consequences of those beliefs." The working goal of the therapist is to help the client to "dispute those irrational beliefs," *D*, and help the client to obtain more rational, helpful beliefs. If REBT is successful, the client gains new behavioral and emotional consequences, symbolized by *E*—a "new, more effective view" (Gilliland & James, 1998; Nelson-Jones, 2000).

REBT attempts to change the client's basic value system (Hansen et al., 1993), and the ultimate consequence is for the client to "not just feel better but get better" (Nelson-Jones, 2000, p. 200). As is common with other cognitive-behavioral approaches, the therapist helps the clients "become their own therapists" (Nelson-Jones, 2000, p. 201) so that they may live a rational life, independent of the therapist.

Techniques. It is common for REBT counselors to convey unconditional acceptance. However, a warm relationship is not considered necessary and is certainly not considered sufficient, to effect change. Too much warmth may actually lead to the client's dependence and approval seeking and thus hinder client growth (Gilliland & James, 1998; Nelson-Jones, 2000). Some REBT counselors believe that the relationship between counselor and client is important initially (Hansen et al., 1993). Because the relationship is not the focus, techniques are. The most common technique is teaching: Helpers teach their clients about REBT assumptions and how the consequences of human nature play out in their lives. Helpers focus on teaching clients how to think differently.

One technique common to the process of REBT is confrontation (Ivey et al., 1987; Kottler & Brown, 1992; Nelson-Jones, 2000). However, a wide variety of techniques are used in REBT to help clients identify and change beliefs. Some techniques, such as the disputing of irrational beliefs and bibliotherapy, work primarily in the cognitive area. Affective and behavioral aspects are also addressed, however, and techniques in these areas might include imagery, questioning (e.g., Burnwell & Chen, 2002), role-play (e.g., Sharp & MaCallum, 2005), homework assignments, rational emotive imagery (Wilde, 2008), thought stopping, and skill training (Gilliland & James, 1998; Nelson-Jones, 2000).

REBT and Diversity. Although most validation studies for the pragmatic approaches have focused on CBT, REBT has some empirical support regarding its usefulness with a range of clients. It has been critiqued as difficult for clients with lower intelligence and lower educational levels (Murdock, 2012). It is a straightforward approach that many clients appreciate, but at times is critiqued as being too simple for addressing systemic, culturally oriented difficulties that clients face. As with other pragmatic approaches, if the therapist is diligent in looking at the thought patterns of clients from the clients' cultural perspectives, therapy should be effective.

Reality Therapy

Most people would love to have every one of their needs met to complete satiation and at all times. However, one big, ever-present force stands in the way—reality. Reality therapists focus on helping clients make responsible choices while getting their basic needs met (Glasser, 1998; Prenzlau, 2006; Wubbolding, 2000).

Life Philosophy. Human beings strive to have their needs meet. According to helpers who use reality therapy, human needs fall into five major areas: survival, loving and being loved, power, freedom, fun. To *survive* requires that people have food, water, shelter, and safety. They also have the basic need to *belong*, to give love to others and receive love. People need to feel close to others and to feel others need and want them. Although the needs to survive and to love are important, people have other needs as well. To be playful, have *fun*, and be active in recreation is important to the human mind. People also need control, *power*, and *freedom*. These needs define what it means to be human (Glasser, 1998). Our behaviors are our tools for getting our needs meet.

However, the founder of reality therapy, William Glasser (1998), shared that getting one's needs met is not always possible. People consistently seek to have their needs met in a world where resources are limited, and they cannot have all their needs met completely and consistently. For example, if people consistently work to have their power needs met by taking control of others, by telling others what to do, and by just being bossy in general, they will likely not get other needs met. For example, meeting the need for power in this manner would likely hinder one's ability to give and receive love.

The effectiveness of human beings is ultimately based on their decisions. Almost every scenario presents people with choices, and their ability to make choices that meet their basic needs determines their level of health. At the two extremes of a continuum are those who can meet their needs in socially appropriate ways, or a *Success Identity*, and those who cannot, or a *Failure Identity*. Learning to get one's needs met is not a guarantee that they will be met. Children learn that the best way to get food is to cry. If an infant's stomach is empty due to lack of food, she cries, and the parents would inevitably take care of the infant's needs. Crying worked. Now, if an adult tried that same approach, perhaps in a faculty meeting, he would likely be met with some strange stares. A reality therapist would assist him in learning what his fundamental needs are and the effective ways to get them met.

Goals of Therapy. The primary goal of reality therapy is to help clients make effective choices, a process that requires the assistance of the helper. A necessary goal of therapy is helping clients to accept responsibility. Making choices requires that clients accept their own role in making change (Glasser, 1965). Clients often want change but do not want to do the work. They must realize what their own role is in creating change.

Understanding is also a driving goal. The helper must assist clients in understanding their own needs. What do the clients want? For most, the basic answer to this question is "something different." However, each individual has different desires within the basic human needs. Identifying these needs and wants is crucial to making new choices.

Techniques. How can counselors help? First, the helper must form a relationship with the client. An effective working relationship requires a helper who offers the client support. The helper should also be nonjudgmental. As a helper, you will likely have different needs and make different choices from your clients. First, you must understand that your clients' choices make sense to them. They believe their decisions are the best way for them to get their needs met. At some point, their behaviors were likely rewarded, but they just are no longer working.

Reality therapists have several signature techniques. First, they often use *contracts* and *plans* with clients, which help clients to articulate specifically what they plan to do to make changes in their lives. Another common technique is termed *pinning down*, which is an essential process in helping the client to be specific in when and how he will follow through with a plan. For example, if Kim asks Duane to "contact the accountant for our private practice," he will respond, "I will." However, she is wise and knows Duane will never do it based on his response. As an individual seated in reality, she then asks, "When?" She is following the principles of reality therapy. For example, if a client shares that she will start taking medicine, as a helper you may explore when, with what doctor, and even how it will be financed.

An additional reality strategy is to encourage clients to adopt *positive-addicting behaviors*, which are behaviors that are so important in people's lives that without them they feel a void. Praying, meditating, exercising, helping others, and volunteering are all examples of behaviors that serve people in socially appropriate ways, fill voids in their lives, and become meaningful to them. Clients who are successful in achieving positive-addicting behaviors are more resilient when they are faced with challenges. Positive-addicting behaviors serve to provide clients with greater tolerance when they are faced with situations that challenge their ability to satisfy basic needs (Glasser, 1965). Contemporary reality therapists offer the *WDEP system* (Wubbolding, 2000). This sequential process has the therapist first help clients recognize their wants (W), evaluate their behavior and what they are doing (D), evaluate (E) themselves to see their present behavior and where it is moving them, and finally to make plans (P) to help clients improve how they get their needs and wants. This process is used to help clients make change and understand what they must do to make change happen.

Reality Therapy and Diversity. Reality therapy continues to be used with a wide variety of clients from many cultures. Reality therapy puts the focus on the individual making change, so it may sometimes minimize the experience clients from minority cultures may experience through oppression, racism, and prejudice. However, if the therapist acknowledges the real disadvantages some minorities face and helps them to make change and adapt to these realties, therapy can be effective with diverse clients.

Reality, Being a Student, and the Intentional Theory Selection Model. A graduate student in psychology came to Kim complaining about feeling "depressed and burned out." He complained that all he did was study and work. He was feeling "out of balance," and life was not giving him what he wanted. He came in for several

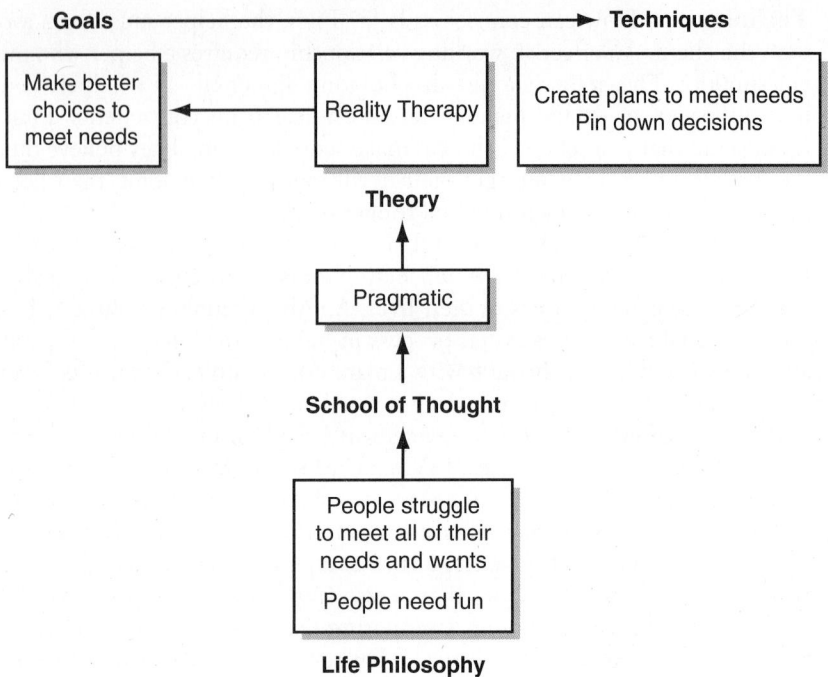

FIGURE 4.4 A Graduate Student's ITS Model

sessions, and then, for the fourth session, he came in smiling, saying he had "figured it out." He described how, after reading a chapter on reality therapy, he realized that he was not making "good choices" in meeting his life "needs and wants." He said, "I have forgotten to play." His ITS now includes his life philosophy of "people struggle to meet all of their needs and wants" and "people need fun" (see Figure 4.4).

CONSTRUCTIVIST SCHOOL OF THOUGHT

As information and research on counseling are collected, new helping theories emerge. These approaches often include aspects of previously founded theories. Currently, contemporary approaches tend to be heavily focused on phenomenology, human uniqueness, multicultural concerns, and client empowerment. Although it has been given different names, we have chosen to refer to this school of thought as constructivist. Others refer to several of these approaches as postmodern (e.g., Corey, 2004), social-constructivist, contemporary (e.g., Halbur & Halbur, 2006), and emerging.

Constructivist counselors typically focus on the meaning and knowledge clients attribute to their experiences. The four approaches we present are not always considered complete theories that stand on their own in a therapy session but rather paradigms that may be incorporated into existing theories. Inherent in many constructivist and contemporary approaches are the common themes of advocacy and prevention. The four theories highlighted in this school are multicultural counseling and therapy, feminist therapy, narrative therapy, and solution-focused brief therapy (SFBT).

Multicultural Counseling and Therapy

Often presented as a unique and independent approach, multicultural counseling and therapy (MCT) is a contemporary answer to working in diverse world; however, it can be utilized as a separate theory or incorporated into existing theories (Corey, 2012). Research demonstrates that being aware of multicultural issues is important in the counseling relationship (e.g., Li, Kim, & O'Brien, 2007). However, it is important to focus not only on clients' individual values and beliefs but also on those of the therapist.

Life Philosophy. The need for MCT arises from the Western European basis of many theories of counseling and psychotherapy (Sue & Sue, 2003). As a result, clients from minority groups may not share the worldview inherent in many traditional theories. Culture must be examined in the counseling and psychotherapy realm (Sue & Sue, 2003) because it serves as an important determinant of who clients were, are, and will become. "All learning is culturally defined and comprehended" (Pedersen & Ivey, 1993, p. 26), as is one's own identity. Counselors who are culturally competent frequently address specific dimensions of culture, including power distance, degree of individualism or collectivism, levels of uncertainty avoidance, trust and mistrust, and masculinity and femininity (Pedersen, Draguns, Lonner, & Trimble, 1996; Sue & Sue, 2003).

Counselors who use MCT value the importance of cultural identity and its development (Ivey et al., 1987; Pedersen et al., 1996) and believe that ethnicity is an important aspect of meaning in personal belief systems (Nichols & Schwartz, 2001). Consequently, the MCT approach was developed in response to the critique that some mainstream theories propose worldviews that are too individualistic to serve all clients effectively (Pedersen et al., 1996).

Counselors who incorporate the MCT approach into their clinical repertoire firmly believe that the presence of an alternative worldview, background, or culture does not necessarily indicate pathology (Nichols & Schwartz, 2001). Culturally competent counselors are aware that problems, concerns, and communication patterns may differ across cultures, and they are skilled at recognizing and treating culture-bound disorders (Pedersen et. al., 1996; Sue & Sue, 2003). Problems may be external rather than internal to the client. For example, the problem might be racism in society (Ivey et al., 1987) rather than an individual being "pathological" or paranoid.

Goals of Therapy. A culturally competent therapist has the awareness, skills, and knowledge needed to address cultural issues and their intersection in the therapeutic process. Often, the first and foremost goal of multicultural counseling is cultural awareness. Effective multicultural helpers are aware of their own cultural values and biases and how they may be detrimental to the counseling relationship (Gilliland & James, 1998; Pedersen & Ivey, 1993; Sue & Sue, 2003). Therefore, pluralist-minded therapists must strive not only to understand their clients' worldviews but also to have a consistent life goal of self-understanding. In addition, helpers must have an understanding of how their own cultural identity adds complexity to the therapeutic relationship. Therapists with cultural awareness view dissimilarities between themselves and their clients as comfortable differences, not deficits (Sue & Sue 2003).

Culturally competent counselors possess knowledge of worldviews other than their own (Sue & Sue, 2003). The goal of awareness is complicated because counselor interventions are based on knowledge of the specific culture of the client and institutional barriers that might affect the client (Pedersen & Ivey, 1993). Being knowledgeable about cultures other than one's own may entail what is called cultural role taking, whereby the therapist "acquires practical knowledge concerning the scope and nature of the client's cultural background, daily living experience, hopes, fears, and aspirations" (Sue & Sue, 2003, p. 20). Inherent in the process of cultural role taking is an understanding of the sociopolitical influences and institutional barriers in the lives of clients from diverse backgrounds (Sue & Sue, 2003).

In addition to awareness and knowledge, appropriate and effective skills and interventions are necessary components of MCT. Culturally competent counselors must have the ability to generate both verbal and nonverbal communication because of the various ways diverse groups may value communication (Sue & Sue, 2003). For example, in some Native American cultures, families share their stories and history through storytelling. This norm may alter how a therapist gathers information from a client from this culture. In addition to being able to communicate in a variety of ways, culturally competent counselors may need to play various roles within the counseling realm. These roles may include consultant and advocate if the clients' needs so dictate.

The MCT approach has implications that move beyond the therapy hour. Counselors who utilize an MCT approach often work to change oppressive systems (Pedersen & Ivey, 1993). Counselors may serve as advocates who not only initiate client change but also reach out on political and sociological levels.

Techniques. A major technique in the MCT approach centers on the role of the counselor, who must consistently consider the client's worldview, background, and culture (Ivey et al., 1987; Pedersen et al., 1996). Effective counseling requires that counselors be aware of how their skills and interventions might be perceived differently by different groups of people (Ivey et al., 1987; Pedersen & Ivey, 1993). Counseling skills and techniques are often appropriate only for specific populations. Thus, helpers have the difficult job of anticipating how a specific technique will affect clients.

Multicultural counselors must be wise consumers of previous research and remember that many interventions "proven" to work have had limited testing in certain populations. Counselors must maintain flexibility and work to reframe or revise definitions of basic concepts such as empathy, health, and growth (Pedersen et al., 1996). They may even need to modify or vary techniques that will address clients of various cultural backgrounds more effectively (Pedersen et al., 1996; Pedersen & Ivey, 1993). Effective helpers do not have to "throw out" their own personal theory or techniques that have been effective in the past. Rather, after gauging their own worldview and that of their clients, they do need to be culturally appropriate in meeting the clients' needs. This difficult task is vital to effective multicultural counseling and psychotherapy.

Multicultural Counseling Therapy and Diversity. It may almost seem silly or redundant to comment on how MCT works in a diverse world and specifically when counseling clients from diverse backgrounds. However, several critiques can be made. First, MCT's primary focus has been on how to work with clients from diverse backgrounds. However, counselors themselves come from diverse backgrounds and there is little commentary or research on how this affects counseling relationships. MCT has been criticized at times for creating cultural divides that are unnecessary. Clients from diverse backgrounds still have universal challenges in their affective worlds and mental health. Multicultural counselors and therapists must be careful not to turn clients' concerns into multicultural issues when diversity may not be a component of the problem presented.

Feminist Therapy

Feminist theories are not unique to the field of counseling and can be found in the fields of philosophy and gender studies as well as art, film, literature, and many other areas. However, feminist theory emphasizes empowerment and advocacy and is becoming increasingly integrated within the helping professions.

Life Philosophy. Like the multicultural approach to counseling and psychotherapy, feminist therapy can stand as a unique theory but is often integrated into other theoretical approaches in practice. Feminist theory examines oppressive sociological trends and how they relate to defined problems and pathology of women. This approach has a variety of beliefs that are often categorized as radical, liberal, social, and cultural (Enns, 1993). However, a common belief of feminist helpers is that our established patriarchal systems subjugate women and either create or support the psychological and sociological challenges women face (Brown & Bryan, 2007; Corey, 2004; Ivey et al., 1987; Nichols & Schwartz, 2001). Newer approaches to feminist therapy are often identified as postmodern, supporting the inclusion of feminist therapy as a social constructivist approach (Murdock, 2009).

Feminist therapists focus on the implications of gender issues (Murdock, 2009; Nichols & Schwartz, 2001) and shed light on the importance of reproductive, biological, and violence issues that play roles in women's lives. Feminist theory also strives to maintain a positive attitude toward women (Corey, 2004) and views the historical female characteristics of connection and caring as strengths rather than weaknesses. Feminist theory finds that problems tend to lie in the social-cultural context and result specifically from a patriarchal society (Corey, 2004; Ivey et al., 1987; Nichols & Schwartz, 2001). This approach deems that external forces such as oppression, discrimination, and harassment—rather than a client's internal shortcomings—may be the source of many disorders and psychological stress. Thus, the therapist must understand that client concerns do not happen in isolation.

Feminist theories and the therapies that emerge from them differ in their focus. There are many different feminist theories and thus many different types of therapy. Although there are commonalities across the philosophies, there are also differences. In the fields of counseling and psychotherapy, the three most common feminist therapies are radical feminism, cultural feminism, and liberal feminism.

Radical feminism is the most historic and often the most controversial feminist approach. It started the feminism movement both socially and in the field of counseling. Radical feminism focuses on the inequality between men and women and the ongoing oppression of women. Often, the deconstruction of patriarchal dominance is of great concern to radical feminists.

Cultural feminists tend to look more at the positive components of the roles women play in society. The tendency is to look at women and men and examine their differences. Through this process women's roles as nurturing and caring, for example (Enns, 1993), are valued and promoted.

Liberal feminists, on the other hand, attempt to minimize the differences between women and men. Most liberal feminists acknowledge that men and women are both capable of similar successes and struggles and that, in bias-free environments, men and women behavior similarly.

Goals of Therapy. The main goal of feminist theory is to help clients see the world in a variety of ways and provide them with choices that allow them to live authentically (Enns, 1993; Ivey et al., 2002; Mancoske, Standifer, & Cauley, 1994; Matsuyuki, 1998). Another driving goal of feminist therapy is to deconstruct traditional patriarchal culture and to establish and strengthen egalitarian, women-supported roles (Corey, 2012). In this pursuit, feminist helpers also strive to encourage and support interdependence (Ivey et al., 1987) as opposed to the goal of independence found in more traditional, historical approaches. In this process, feminist helpers strive to give women alternatives to the roles they play (Mancoske et al., 1994). Additional goals may depend on the type of feminist therapy being offered; thus, feminist counselors may have the goals of social change, empowerment, and building women's roles (Halbur & Halbur, 2011).

Techniques. As the basis of the counseling process, the feminist therapist must form an egalitarian relationship with the client. However important this relationship may be, the feminist therapist also actively utilizes community resources, participates in therapy, gives information, and provides personal validation (Ivey et al., 1987). In general, counselors have a similar and necessary repertoire of skills across the various theoretical approaches. However, feminist helpers must also strive to listen attentively, honor their clients, challenge stereotypes, and support equality (Corey, 2004, 2012).

Feminist helpers typically serve in a collaborative role, strive to validate clients, and support the development of women within society (Corey, 2004; Ivey et al., 1987). As a political and social approach, counselors move beyond the therapy hour, often striving to make larger changes, like counselors using the MCT approach. Feminist theory is based in part on the notion that the personal is political and that oppression occurs in many forms. As noted earlier, the theory deems that external forces, such as oppression, discrimination, and harassment rather than a client's internal deficiencies, may be the source of many disorders and psychological stress. Thus, examining and evaluating social structures and biases comprise a technique that is often used during therapy (Nichols & Schwartz, 2001), as is raising consciousness about difficulties that may be due to prescribed gender roles. Therapy may also include taking action to eliminate injustice rather than adjusting to the world as it is (Ivey et al., 1987; Murdock, 2009).

Although advocacy as a general technique is common in feminist approaches, other modalities such as *empowerment feminist therapy* and *androgyny and assertiveness training* are common techniques used by feminist counselors.

To complicate matters, techniques vary greatly depending on which style of therapy is used. For example, in liberal feminist therapy, the focus is often to "minimize the differences between men and women and to assume that within bias-free environments, men and women will behave similarly" (Enns, 1993, p. 45). A cultural feminist would attempt to "emphasize differences between men and women and place special importance on the development of nurturing, cooperative, interpersonal qualities within society" (Enns, 1993, p. 46). Although the various styles of feminist therapy rely on unique techniques, their underlying philosophies and goals are similar.

Feminist Therapy and Diversity. At first glance, it would seem that feminist therapies should be ready to help a pluralistic society. Feminist therapists are keenly aware of how culture affects, and sometimes even pathologizes, individuals—especially women. Depending on the style of feminism utilized, there can be value struggles with diverse clients. For example, *radical feminism* focuses on deconstructing patriarchal roles. Female clients who are in traditionally feminine roles or who want to move into traditional roles may be uncomfortable working with a therapist who focuses so greatly on empowerment and interdependence. However, a female who wants a more traditionally feminine role in some aspects of her life, may feel understood by a *cultural feminist* who celebrates the nurturing role some traditional women's roles require.

Feminist approaches have been critiqued as not being beneficial to male clients. However, many men have had great counseling experiences with feminist therapists using *gender-neutral counseling*. Feminist therapy can be very effective; however, therapists must be intentional, understand the values of their clients, and avoid imposing their own values.

Feminist Theory and the Intentional Theory Selection Model. The ITS of a feminist might look unique because he might utilize various techniques to meet the major goals of this philosophical approach. For example, a feminist therapist with whom Kim recently talked shared that he believes many of his clients with eating disorders struggle due to "society norms of what is attractive." He believes that his clients struggle to mirror media and sociological icons but fail because these icons are not typically realistic. Many of his clients struggle not just with unhealthy eating behaviors but also with issues of self-esteem. He articulated what his ITS might look like (see Figure 4.5).

Narrative Therapy

Narrative therapy and its contemporary popularity are attributed primarily to the work of Michael White (2007). Narrative therapists believe that healing and change can occur through conversations—through the telling and retelling of stories.

Life Philosophy. Ultimately, narrative helpers believe that, as individuals, people make sense of their everyday lives through narratives (Rosen & Kuehlwein, 1996;

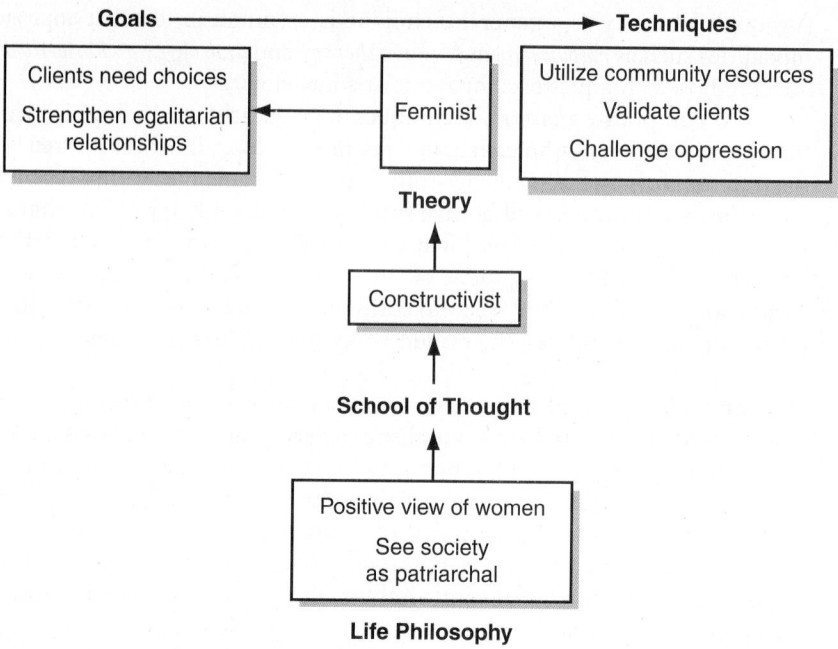

FIGURE 4.5 A Feminist's ITS Model

Russell, Van de Brock, Adams, Rosenberger, & Essig, 1993). These stories include what people want, what they like about themselves, and even what they want to change. They define themselves fundamentally through the stories they share. They may share stories of themselves as a son, daughter, parent, partner, and so on. The stories they choose to tell reveal much about who they are.

Narrative therapists also believe that people are social creatures and that much of what they describe as paramount in their narratives occurs within relationships. Consequently, therapists must understand clients in a social context. Narrative therapists believe that personal experience is ambiguous and may be understood and interpreted in multiple ways, and they believe that the stories people tell themselves are important in determining how they will act (Nichols & Schwartz, 2001).

Narrative helpers take a rather positive view of humans. They tend to see the best in people, and typically believe that people have good intentions (Nichols & Schwartz, 2001) and strive to live in a "good" way. Of course, this approach is subjective; there is no right or wrong, good or bad, and especially normal or abnormal.

Narrative helpers are social constructivists who believe people are greatly influenced by their culture and environment (Corey, 2004; Murdock, 2009). Narrative theorists believe that the truth of experience is created rather than discovered (Nichols & Schwartz, 2001); consequently, they believe that truly understanding others requires seeing how others view the past, present, and future (Nichols & Schwartz, 2001; Zimmerman & Dickerson, 1996).

Goals of Therapy. The goal of narrative therapy is not just to solve problems but also to change the client's whole way of thinking and living (Nichols & Schwartz, 2001). Problems are external to the individual and occur consistently. The therapist must help the individual be prepared for the future and not simply offer a therapeutic bandage for the current pain the client faces.

People tell others and themselves who they are through stories of their own lives and experiences. The stories help define where they have been and what they have done on the way to becoming who they are. If you tell someone who you are by sharing stories of glory, you define yourself as confident. If you instead tell someone who you are by your defeats, you share a person defined by failure. As helpers, you cannot change the past, but you can help clients *restory*, or tell their life story in a new way.

As people develop, they all have experiences that shape their stories. For example, when Duane was 5, he started wearing glasses, and he also won his first award—most creative fire-safety poster. When he was 12, he was picked on by a few boys for wearing the wrong shoes, and he was given an award for outstanding computer skills. Each of these events had a personal, subjective meaning attached to it for Duane. If he entered therapy and said, "I feel like a successful person," which events do you think he used to define himself? Likely, he would describe himself through successes: He won awards when he was 5 and 12. However, if he entered therapy and said, "I am different," he likely defined himself by those experiences that separated him: wearing big glasses and funny shoes. If he entered therapy defining himself as *different*, your goal may likely be to help him restory and define himself as *successful*.

Techniques. The narrative therapist serves as a collaborator. Like a driver education instructor, the therapist is along for the ride and may even give directions, but the client has hold of the wheel. In this process, the counselor is active, often asking many questions to aid in the client's understanding. The therapist is also active in discovering and articulating client strengths, often looking for exceptions in the client's story. *Exceptions* occur when clients share experiences that are contrary to how they are defining their story. For example, if a client describes himself as being unassertive but then shares a time he stood up to someone, the therapist sees an exception. By identifying this exception for the client, the therapist can help him begin to see himself in a new way.

Some write that the basic goals of narrative counseling are to increase clients' choices, to coauthor new stories while helping clients view themselves in a new way, and to transform clients' identity (e.g., Nichols & Schwartz, 2001). In this process, the helper must develop an initial narrative that externalizes and personifies the problem, seek unique outcomes, deconstruct the story, develop a new story or life narrative, and reinforce the client's new story (Corey, 2004; Nichols & Schwartz, 2001). However, narrative therapists often consider *externalization* to be the most important technique they use (Cashin, 2008; Rosen & Kuehlwein, 1996; Weist, Wong, Brotherton, & Cervantes, 2001). Effective narrative therapists help their clients to see that their problems exist outside themselves (Corey, 2004; Nichols & Schwartz, 2001), which allows clients to be separated from their problems instead of defined by them. This approach also "allows conflict to decrease, lessens the sense of failure, encourages the client to struggle against the problem, opens new possibilities, and creates dialogue" (Weist et al. 2001, p. 5).

Of course, an additional major technique of the narrative helper is to promote storytelling, which, for many people, is therapeutic in and of itself; clients gain relief through their own sharing. For other clients, however, storytelling is simply a necessary step to begin doing therapeutic work (Rosen & Kuehlwein, 1996) that often includes the use of *metaphors* as a powerful tool. The client should end therapy with a new story, a story defining self in positive, healthy ways.

Narrative Approach and Diversity. The narrative approach to counseling is rooted in social constructivism. Clients are viewed in the context of their culture and how they attribute meaning to their personal experience. Narrative therapy attempts to allow the clients to be the experts on their lives. This invites a multiculturally sensitive relationship. Because clients are the experts on their lives, however, some cultures and individuals will struggle with the therapist's potential lack of direction. This challenge may be overcome when therapists remind clients that the therapist is the expert on the therapeutic process (Corey, 2012).

Solution-Focused Brief Therapy

In the days of Freud, therapy was often five times a week and lasted for many years. As you can imagine, this would not get much support from most contemporary insurance companies! However, solution-focused brief therapy makes the assumption that change can be facilitated effectively and quickly.

Life Philosophy. Solution-focused brief therapy, with its many different names and diverse founders (e.g., Berg, 2003; de Shazer, 1985), is becoming vastly popular as a time-sensitive approach. Helpers practicing in this paradigm believe that specific changes can occur in a brief time when that time is focused. On day one of therapy, the solution-focused helper gathers information from clients to learn what changes they want to occur. Solution-oriented helpers speak little about the etiology of problems. The focus of solution-oriented approaches is defining the problem, not determining why it exists.

One of the best descriptions comes from Gilliland and James (1998), who state that solution-focused brief therapy is "a person-centered, behavioral stew with a dash of cognitive-behaviorism thrown in for good measure" (p. 309). Helpers in this paradigm do not direct their clients to make change that is valued by the therapist. Instead, the helper stays focused on the future and assists clients in finding those areas that they want changed.

Similar to helpers using the humanistic approaches, solution-focused helpers understand that their worldview is different from their clients' view. A client's behaviors and emotions truly make sense only from that individual's unique perspective. Consequently, a phenomenological approach is vital to therapy.

Solution-focused helpers believe that one key component of therapy is first to determine what an individual is doing that is contributing to the problem. Clients often do not realize, or do not articulate, what they do to actively make their problem or problems continue. This vital question is often the first one that solution-focused helpers try to answer. A second belief is that knowing where one wants to go makes getting there much more likely. People can easily get lost if they do not know their destination. The solution-focused helper first helps clients realize where they want to go because, without that knowledge, direction cannot be found.

Goals of Therapy. Quite simply, the paramount goal of solution-focused brief therapy is to assist clients in finding their unique solutions. In solution work, the goal is to see what needs to change for the specific client and then to make that happen. Therapy is focused and specific about what change needs to occur and attempts to fix only what needs fixing. The goals for clients vary because each client is unique and so will be their solutions.

Techniques. Imagine that this text is magic and that, after reading it, you would be the therapist you always wanted to be. Knowing what would happen, how would you be different than you are today? This variation of the *miracle question* typifies a paramount technique in the solution-focused approach. The question moves immediately to seeing what the client wants to be different. The miracle question (e.g., Lloyd & Dallos, 2006) is often asked the first day in therapy because it helps clients move to a future orientation, where their problems have already changed and hopefully disappeared. "If I could give you a magic pill that would change your life to be exactly how you want it, what would your life look like?" This question and others like it assist helpers in seeing where clients want to go. They are based on the assumption that, in therapy, knowing where to go makes getting there much easier.

The solution-focused helper also looks for *exceptions* in the client's story. Exceptions are components in clients' stories that do not fit the problem they are sharing. For example, Kim worked with a client who knew she was a therapist and professor. He stated, "I have little empathy and want to change that." One day in session, when he knew finals week was quickly approaching, he stated, "I bet this is a tough time of the semester for you." Kim smiled and pointed out his empathetic statement as an exception to his story. Helping clients identify these exceptions helps them see their own ability to change.

Helpers also look for and help clients find personal strengths. This *strength assessment* is vital because it helps clients see their own resources, which they can include in the process of change. This process of empowerment helps clients focus on their goals and their abilities and resources that can aid in achieving those goals.

The solution-focused brief helper first attempts to build a therapeutic relationship. If successful, the therapist moves immediately to helping the client see what she wants to change and how life can be different. Then, armed with techniques, the therapist helps the client gain insight and move to action. Therapy focuses not on the briefness of the therapy but on the immediate alleviation of the problems the client faces.

SFBT and Diversity. In general, SFBT is considered effective with a wide range of clients. Individuals from diverse backgrounds come to therapy wanting change. However, SFBT may be a challenge for clients from cultures that want to avoid problem saturation in their narrative and in the counseling relationship. SFBT promotes respect for all clients and an understanding of clients' cultural and social contexts, so it can be used effectively with most clients.

FAMILY APPROACHES SCHOOL OF THOUGHT

Separating family therapies from those previously presented is a major challenge for several reasons. A major confounding issue is that all of the theories previously addressed in this text have family applications; techniques; and, at times, complete family theories that expand on their individual approaches. Several theorists' approaches, such as Adler's analytic approach (e.g., Corey, 2004; Dinkmeyer, 2007) and Roger's person-centered approach (e.g., Snyder, 2002), have commonly been presented as family theories. Other approaches are often difficult to separate from family approaches, as is the case with narrative therapy, which continues to gain acceptance as a family therapy approach (Saltzburg, 2007). Therapies not typically considered family therapies, such as Logotherapy (e.g., Lantz, 1989), also have support for their importance as family approaches.

Family theories and therapies that are iconic in the field have some differences, however. Most family therapies are referred to as *systemic*. The family is considered a systemic unit, and change of one family member will cause the rest of the system and its members to change. Thus, there is little focus on individual development, personality structures, or pathology. There is often a rejection of the traditional approach of an *identified patient* that serves as the focus of therapy. Instead, the family as a whole is viewed as "the client." The interactions of the family are considered the causes of individual systems, and to create change, the family must change. For the purpose of this text, we present Bowen family systems theory, strategic family therapy, and structural family therapy. However, there are many other theories of family therapy, such as experiential, symbolic, communication, and Milan strategic theories (e.g., Goldenberg & Goldenberg, 2008; Nichols, 2008), that offer richness to the family therapy school of thought.

Bowen Family Systems Therapy

Murray Bowen is iconic in the development of transgenerational models of family therapy. His approach is often referred to as *family systems theory, transgenerational*, or just simply *Bowenian*. His approach provides much of the "scaffolding" of many historical and contemporary family therapies (Goldenberg & Goldenberg, 2008, p. 175) and is a seminal approach to family therapy.

Life Philosophy. Bowen was greatly affected by the psychodynamic approach and believed that the relationship between child and mother was of great importance. However, he believed that parents, like their parents before, pass on their emotional struggles, such as their anxieties. He observed that families exist as unique, collective emotional systems. He believed that, within any family system, there are various processes that interact to tie family members together and to separate them. There are two opposing forces: one moving family members closer and one moving them farther apart (Bowen, 1966; Ivey, Ivey, D'Andrea, & Simek-Morgan, 2007).

Central to family functioning is the degree to which *self-differentiation* occurs and presents within each member of the family. The term *self-differentiation* is used to describe how people react to their emotions. Those who are too undifferentiated respond quickly to emotions. Their emotions become hard for them to separate from their actions and beliefs. Bowen believed that levels of differentiation greatly affected the multigenerational transmission of anxieties and dysfunction in a family.

Bowen believed that patterns occur in families across generations. Values, religious behavior, dysfunction, gender roles, and even occupational similarities can be viewed across generations to help understand the presenting family. Consequently, his philosophy was focused on the present and how the past has surfaced.

Goals of Therapy. Bowenian goals of therapy involve changing the family as a system. A major goal of therapy is to help individual family members increase their levels of differentiation (Ivey et al., 2007), allowing them to be more autonomous and emotionally mature. An additional primary goal is to manage emotions (Goldenberg & Goldenberg, 2008) within the family, thus helping to reduce symptoms and emotional turmoil. In attempting these endeavors, a common additional goal is to provide boundary clarification between family members. The family serves as an emotional unit and consequently at times experiences internal conflict. Bowen first presented what are still commonly called *triangles*. He observed that, when there is conflict or anxiety involving two family members, there is an attempt to draw in a third person to diffuse some of the negative energy. Often, these triangles are ineffective, so a goal of therapy is to identify these triangles.

Techniques. A major technique of Bowen family systems therapy arises out of the view that problems are most often the result of multigenerational patterns. The *genogram* is used to identify, discuss, and assess the family patterns. Genograms are created with the family to develop a picture of typically at least three generations (Gerson, McGoldrick, & Petry, 2008). The goal is to help families to understand and change patterns by viewing marriages, health concerns, religious patterns, and triangles.

Bowen did believe in remaining objective in therapy (in sharp contrast to other later family theories). He believed it is important, at times, to avoid entering into triangles within the family or couple with whom he was working. He believed that this objectivity would show family members what a healthy relationship with functional boundaries would look like.

Typically, however, Bowen did not identify many techniques. He believed that questioning the family members to understand family history was important and that the counselor providing hypotheses would help the family gain great knowledge of its own patterns and emotional system.

Strategic Family Therapy

Jay Haley and Milton Erikson are two of the most prominent names associated with strategic family therapy. The strategic approach focuses on changing repetitive patterns that create present problems in the family. It is an active, directive, and typically brief systemic approach.

Life Philosophy. Strategic therapists believe it is important to focus on present problems in the family. There is little talk of a "life philosophy" because this approach does not emphasize individual development or personality construction. Instead, strategic therapists focus on removing problems that are occurring now.

Strategic therapists, like others, are concerned with making change. However, change is viewed in several ways. Some changes are really *first-order changes*, which means that the specific behavior or concern is alleviated. Change occurs in a linear fashion. However, strategic therapists recognize that greater change results when *second-order changes* occur. Second-order changes focus on changing the rules of the family (Nichols, 2008), which allows for change that is meaningful and lasting.

The family approach, as a systemic approach, rarely focuses on personal growth (Goldenberg & Goldenberg, 2008) or individual needs (Haley, 1991). The family is a complete system with dysfunctional behaviors that serve to keep it in a state of homeostasis. Consequently, families as systems resist change. The philosophy of the therapist is that change can happen and that, through creative and new solutions, the family will acquire new rules and new, healthier patterns.

Goals of Therapy. The goal of therapy, on the one hand, is rather simple. It is to change family patterns intentionally. Specific movements within the strategic approach, for example, the Mental Research Institute (MRI), have also identified potential goals such as defining family complaints, learning how the family has attempted to alleviate problems, and understanding the family's communication in describing problems (Nichols, 2008). Goals vary greatly, however, because therapy and the specific techniques are considered unique for each family. Once a family's view of the problem is understood, the therapist's main goal is to eliminate or change the problem as presented by the family.

Techniques. Strategic therapists attempt to produce a warm and relaxed environment for therapy to be most effective. Counselors then develop unique interventions specific to the family seeking help. Jay Haley, for example, was especially known for his use of *directives*, which are highly intentional directions or prescriptions that help the family view or change its problems or behaviors in its perpetuating system.

Directives are individually tailored to the specific needs of the presenting family. Therapists' creativity and intentionality are very important.

Paradoxical interventions are indirect ways for the therapist to maneuver around family resistance and help to create change. The MRI approach describes the importance of *prescribing the symptom*. This process may actually involve instructing the family to increase or work harder on its presenting issue. The hope is that the family members learn they have control over the pattern or realize its absurdity. For example, Kim was working with a family in which the son and stepmother were giving each other the "silent treatment." Her assignment for them was to spend the next week not talking at all! Well, they were unsuccessful at not talking—they learned they actually needed each other—and made a huge breakthrough in therapy.

Strategic therapists also utilize *reframing*. This technique requires therapists to describe family problems in a new way. For example, describing "overprotection" as extreme care can help family members view what was previously viewed as overinvolvement as a sign of love. This often allows the process of changing family patterns to begin.

Pretend techniques involve having family members act differently than they normally would under the guise of play (Madanes, 1981). This often helps behaviors change as the family begins to behave in a new way. As you can see, strategic therapists' techniques are highly directive in their attempts to change family patterns in creative new ways.

Structural Family Therapy

Structural family therapy is primarily attributed to the work of Salvador Minuchin. The influence of this approach is easy to see because the constructs and terms are iconic in what professionals and laypeople think of as family therapy.

Life Philosophy. As a systemic approach, structural therapy focuses on the family as a whole. Structural therapists do not typically accept the belief that there are dysfunctional, sick, or psychosomatic individuals. Instead, they focus on dysfunctional, sick, or psychosomatic families. Taking a rather traditional approach, they see much of the difficulty in families as a lost or misconstrued hierarchy within the family. Without an appropriate hierarchy within the structure of the family, there are bound to be problems. Obviously, the structure of the family is of utmost importance, and the philosophy of this approach is to understand and even join the many subsystems that may occur in a family. For example, parents, children, females, or even the socially minded individuals in a family may develop *subsystems* that perpetuate the functioning of the family—perhaps in positive or negative ways. Within the family, *boundaries* describe the psychological closeness of members, and *permeability* describes how easily members can cross into other subsystems. Members of a family with boundaries that are weak are *enmeshed* through overinvolvement in each other's lives (Goldenberg & Goldenberg, 2008). However, members of a family with strict, overly rigid boundaries are *disengaged*. Different boundaries may exist for different family members and different subsystems.

Goals of Therapy. The philosophy or view for the family from a structuralist's point of view makes the goals seem rather commonsense. Understanding the structure and hierarchy of the presenting family is extremely important. There is a key assumption that the coping mechanisms and hierarchy of the family are no longer working and must be changed. Developing a healthy structure for the family is important. In this process, it is important to define and develop *healthy boundaries*. To maintain a healthy structure, *appropriate alignments* should also be developed. For example, in the face of family discord and couple conflicts, it is not uncommon for a parent to develop alignments with his children and not his spouse. As a result, a goal of therapy might be to develop a spousal alignment. Changing the family means changing the structure, the hierarchy, and the *transactional patterns*. The ultimate goal of therapy is to create a family system that is healthier, with patterns that lead to healthy family functioning.

Techniques. There are a multitude of identified skills and techniques within structural therapy (e.g., Figley & Nelson, 1990). A key technique or role of the therapist is *joining and accommodating* the family, which is a process of becoming like a family member, relating (joining) and adjusting (accommodating) to the family's style and mannerisms (Minuchin, 1974).

Family mapping (see Minuchin, 1974, for a description) helps to clarify the structure of the family and to assess where change needs to occur. The family map is a graphic representation of the family's coalitions, subsystems, affiliations, and power. Mapping makes it easier to do *boundary making*, which is a process of realigning and changing psychological boundaries within the family and between family subsystems. Sometimes it becomes important to loosen or tighten boundaries between family members and to use *unbalancing*, a technique the therapist uses to change the relationships between family members by providing greater support to one member (Goldenberg & Goldenberg, 2008) and allowing change to occur. Although there are a variety of other techniques, two main techniques aimed at changing the transactional patterns of the family are enactment and reframing. *Enactment* is an attempt to have family members bring into the session a conflict, problem, or situation that occurs outside the session. *Reframing*, is similar to reframing in strategic family therapy. It is an attempt to redefine family behaviors to keep the family together as a functioning unit. Giving new meaning to behaviors allows members to change their patterns.

A Family Therapist and the Intentional Theory Selection Model. Rosa had been a practicing psychologist for several years. She considered herself a cognitive-behavioral therapist but was challenged by the fact that much of the change she attempted with clients was thwarted by their families. Her caseload was becoming filled with couples and families, so she attended a workshop on contemporary family interventions. The workshop challenged her to use the ITS model to see what family theories might fit best for her. She shared that she felt the clients she worked with would struggle to change unless the "shape" of the family changed. She also shared that she mostly believed change should occur to solve problems currently presented.

SIX SCHOOLS OF THOUGHT AND THEIR THEORIES OF HELPING

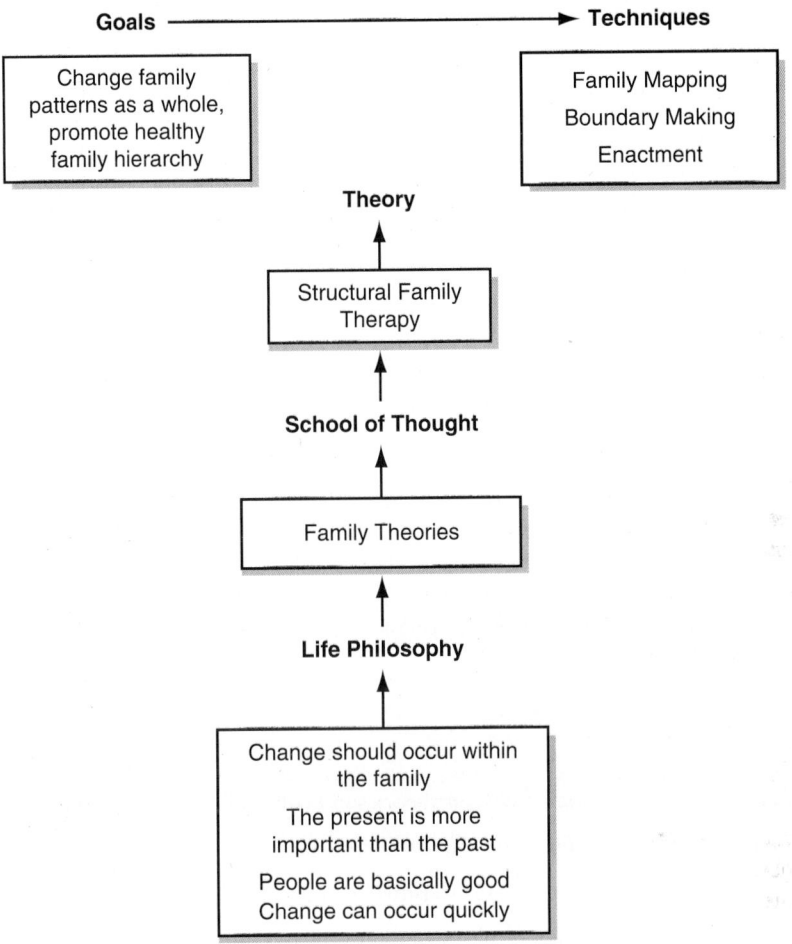

FIGURE 4.6 A Family System ITS Model

Rosa acknowledged that she could find an approach that was more congruent with her beliefs and developed an ITS that looked similar to Figure 4.6.

Family Therapies and Diversity

A discussion of family therapies and their application to diversity would be long because it would have to cover many points showing strengthens and weaknesses. Family therapists should understand that the specific family therapies differ only slightly on how multicultural concepts are ingrained. In general, the strength of family therapies with diverse clients is that the family therapist is already taking a systemic approach that includes family values, rules, and patterns. The addition of cultural values is not that difficult. Traditional family therapies are often critiqued for having a limited definition on what indeed makes a family; however, most family therapists across the board are looking for ways to make their work more inclusive. For example, most training programs have changed the name of family courses from Marriage and Family Counseling to Couples and Family Counseling to include same-sex and cohabitating relationships. More traditional family approaches do run the risk of promoting gender-specific roles and highlighting a nuclear family as the ideal structure. An effective family therapist will be able to take a systemic approach while integrating clients' cultures and family structures.

SUMMARY

Over 15 theories falling into 6 schools of thought were presented in this chapter. Each theory comes from the work of different authors with unique life philosophies that reflect how they intervene and the goals they value in working with families and individuals. The chapter presented some of the most cited, best researched, and most utilized counseling approaches. The included summaries of the various theories can serve as a good reference when you need to be reminded of their key concepts. Chapter 5 offers you examples of professionals and students who have used the ITS model to help them decide which theory is most applicable for them.

REFLECTION QUESTIONS

1. After reading this chapter, which theory or theories did you find most interesting?
2. Which theories were most difficult for you to understand?
3. Which theories seem to be less culturally sensitive to you?
4. In your search to ascertain a theoretical orientation, which theory do you hope to explore in more detail?
5. Which family theory makes the most sense for you, given your life philosophy?

Case Examples for Integrating Theory into Practice

5

As you search to integrate theory into your practice, you might wonder how others have worked through the Intentional Theory Selection (ITS) model of making theory practical. This chapter will provide you with several scenarios where the model can be and has been used. The case studies included in the chapter represent (1) clinicians who have used the model to determine their theoretical orientation, (2) client cases where you will be able to apply the model to shape your theory and plan the helping relationship, and (3) supervision examples where you can apply the model to clinicians seeking supervision from you.

CLINICIAN CASE STUDIES

Now that you have perused the ITS model of making theory practical, you may choose to work through the process for yourself. A cursory reading of most theories textbooks can help you determine the theories you like best. The difficulty for most people occurs, however, when the theory needs to be applied to a client sitting in front of them. This chapter will provide you with the experiences and reflections of four helpers as they worked through the ITS model of selecting a theoretical orientation. Each case is a real account of people in the helping professions who have utilized the ITS model. The helping professionals presented in the cases are diverse in their cultural backgrounds, fields of study, practice settings, and years of experience in the field. Their experiences searching for a theoretical orientation are just as diverse and interesting. After each case study, reflection questions help you better understand the process of developing and solidifying your theoretical orientation.

Case One: Evan

Life Philosophy. Prior to coming to my master's program, I had never really been "forced" to think about or verbalize my life philosophy. I had been through college, obtained a bachelor's degree in family services, and come out of that program still not knowing who I really was and what I wanted out of life. I'm not sure at that time that I even wanted to figure these things out. I felt as if I was just "doing what I was supposed to do." I knew I had been through a lot in my first two years of college: many negative experiences with sex and relationships, alcohol and drug abuse, an abusive relationship, and whittling relationships with friends and family. When I came to this program, I was asked things I had never before been asked—and had never asked myself. I had thought about them sporadically but had never been expected to answer them verbally or in written form. I was asked to define values and morals in general, and I remember this being difficult to do. I was expected to define my own specific personal values, morals, beliefs, and ideas about how the world works. After having gone through the first two years of my three-year program, I had a pretty good idea of what my own specific values, morals, and beliefs were as well as ideas about how the world works.

I think one of the most transforming and difficult processes for me was recording some of my sessions and having others view my recordings and give feedback on my clinical skills. Learning to accept and positively view constructive criticism and feedback is the part of the process that helped me to partially figure out my life philosophy. I remember being crushed and feeling as if I was almost worthless after receiving feedback on my skills during my first few semesters. Now, I try to view the feedback as a necessary stepping-stone to get to where I am today. I now recognize that I needed to go through feeling crushed and almost worthless initially in order to want and appreciate all types of feedback. This process assisted me in defining what things I believe in, how I am, and the type of person I strive to be.

Participating in personal counseling is another factor that aided me in my transformation. My academic program required that I participate in a minimum of five sessions of personal counseling. I wanted to fulfill this requirement, but I also knew deep down inside that I truly needed to get some help. I felt like I was sinking because areas of my life felt out of control. Over a period of two years, I journeyed through the experience of counseling as a client. This process assisted me in defining who I am, my beliefs, and my values. It also greatly helped me to understand how counseling really works. I believe I was partially exposed to a successful counselor-client relationship. I was able to learn the other side of the counselor-client relationship. I experienced the full range of the relationship, from building trust to confrontation to termination. I now truly believe that one does not know how scary, stressful, terrifying, and uncomfortable counseling is for the client unless one has been a client. Without being a client, one also does not know how rewarding and fulfilling counseling can be for the client who has the motivation to change. Throughout this process, I "found" myself and came to believe in myself, thus clarifying my beliefs, morals, values, ideas of how the world works, and life philosophy.

School of Thought. To figure out my school of thought, I first needed to figure out my life philosophy. My own philosophy included my beliefs, morals, values, ideas of how the world works, self-understanding, and what gives meaning to my life. After I had figured out much of my life philosophy, I then began reading about the different schools of thought and deciding which ones fit my way of viewing the world and how I think it works. I tried simultaneously to figure out my life philosophy and into which school of thought it fit. I seemed really to struggle through this process, but it seemed to work out in the end. For the most part, I feel I have now figured it out. As I am nearing the completion of my master's degree, I realize that I have had ample opportunity for introspection.

Theory. I have been able to feel grounded in selecting a theoretical orientation after reading books; taking additional courses; and completing my practical courses, where I gained more experience with clients. I wanted to pick a theory and then try to use it with clients in addition to using the techniques with them. This felt so uncomfortable to me, almost as if I wasn't myself in sessions. It was very frustrating and anxiety provoking because that's how I thought the theory should work and it didn't. I felt like the process was so ambiguous and didn't understand why it had to be "backward." "Trust the process" is what I have continued to hear from professors and have continued to tell myself. What I found was that I needed to have experience being myself with clients and not focusing on what theoretical orientation I was using in sessions. I found that using my own personality and then fitting that style into a theory or theories really worked for me.

Techniques and Goals. I have a base of general techniques and goals I use with each client, but other ones are developed or matched after I have developed a therapeutic relationship with my client. I base techniques on the client's personality and what I think the client will most accept. I may use techniques more directly or more collaboratively with the client. It just seems to depend on the person. The way I figured out that this works best for me was to experiment in sessions with different ideas and techniques. That seemed to be the best way for me to find out practically what seemed to fit.

REFLECTION QUESTIONS

After reading Evan's experience, answer the following questions:

1. What have you learned from Evan's process?
2. What were the key moments in Evan's learning?
3. What were the major transitions in Evan's development as a professional helper?
4. What were your thoughts and feelings as you read Evan's journey?

Case Two: Jill

Life Philosophy. As I have gone through the first building block in making theory practical, I have realized that examining my life philosophy is as complicated as it sounds. Asking questions such as "What is truth?" and "Are people good?" takes courage and motivation. I have found that I must look inside myself to answer these questions and that the answers are true only for me. My ultimate answer to life philosophy has been to realize that mine changes daily and no one else thinks, feels, or views the world in the same way. I find myself examining my life philosophy with each new client who sits in front of me, and it changes, expands, contracts, and shifts based on each new circumstance. I may ask the same questions in each situation, but the answers will inevitably be different. How would I react in this situation? What coping mechanisms would I employ? What are this person's coping mechanisms? Does this person have a support system? What are his or her resources? What are my expectations of this situation based on my unique worldview?

In examining these questions, I have come to the conclusion that I am a person who emphasizes thinking. It is my view that our actions influence our thoughts, and vice versa. Clients may present with distortions of thought, may act before thinking, or may be able to think but not act. Understanding that I place importance on thinking has led me fluidly to the next building block, which is choosing a school of thought.

School of Thought. In examining each school of thought, I have asked the questions "What is it about this school of thought that matches the way I think and feel about the world?" and "Are there components that I feel contradict my views?" In other words, "What can I take from this school of thought and what can I discard?" This is the tedious aspect of choosing theory in that it requires a lot of reading and research. I found myself looking first at the founders of the theory and then branching out to emerging theorists. What I found is that there are aspects of cognitive-behavioral theory that fit my personal style and aspects of humanistic theory that I deem essential. Once I chose these theories, I began to break down these schools of thought and look at individual aspects of each in order to choose a theory.

Theory. Determining a person's theory is a delicate process that can become frustrating. When I first began looking at theory, I had the idea that I needed to agree with all the tenets in order to call it my chosen theory. Through instruction and discussion, I have found that choosing a theory is like choosing a piece of chocolate from a sampler box. A person might choose a piece of chocolate, take a bite, find that he or she does not enjoy the taste, and throw it away. Conversely, a person might choose a piece, take a bite, and find that the piece of chocolate tastes wonderful on the tongue and stimulates the senses. Choosing aspects of theory can be similar in that a person might find an aspect that makes a lightbulb appear above her head or choose a technique that inspires results consistently. As I began to look at cognitive-behavioral and humanistic theories, I found aspects that fit my personality, such as the thinking-behavior connection, the essential component of building a solid therapeutic relationship, and the importance of providing education and opportunities for the client to practice therapeutic techniques outside counseling sessions. Finally, choosing a theory is not a linear process. A person chooses a theory or theories based on his worldview, which evolves over time. My worldview as a new clinician will not be the same as my worldview as a counseling professional with 20 years of experience. My professional and personal experiences will influence my worldview as well as my choice of theory throughout my life.

Goals and Techniques. Once a person chooses aspects of theory that fit her personality, it is easy to choose goals and techniques. I have chosen cognitive-behavioral and humanistic theories as my foundation. Therefore, my therapeutic goals most often center on assisting a person to change behaviors, recognize irrational or unproductive thinking patterns, and process emotions surrounding life events. My techniques often involve providing education for the client, assigning and processing appropriate homework assignments with the client, and assisting the client in exploring emotions and thinking patterns. Goals and techniques need to be flexible, however, and counselors need to realize that they can choose techniques from all schools of thought. Different clients require different interventions, and counselors must be willing to look outside their theory or theories to find suitable goals and techniques.

REFLECTION QUESTIONS

After reading Jill's experience, answer the following questions:

1. What did you learn from Jill's process?
2. What were the major transitions in Jill's development as a professional helper?
3. How was Jill's journey similar to and/or different from Evan's in Case One?
4. What were your thoughts and feelings as you read Jill's journey?
5. Which parts of Jill's story are similar to and/or different from your own?

Case Three: Garrett

I was excited to be able to participate in a workshop offered by the authors of this text because I wanted to find out which theoretical orientation would best fit my approach to counseling as I study to become a counseling psychologist. In my theories of psychotherapy class, we went through each theory and learned a variety of techniques. For my final project, I put a binder together, listing each theory, its theorist, and its techniques. But I was not satisfied. I did not know where to go from there. I knew that I preferred a few theories over others, but I did not know how to go about finding a theoretical orientation that fit for me. Around the same time, I had the opportunity to explore the ITS model with the authors.

As a result of my coursework, I feel that I have the knowledge and skills to counsel, but I just don't know how to put it toward a theoretical orientation. I am currently a therapist at a residential treatment facility, and I feel that a theoretical orientation would help me to guide my clients in a more beneficial way. Some therapists where I work do not use theoretical orientation, but I feel it would help me be more consistent with my clients.

The foundation of the ITS model is life philosophy, what gives meaning to my life. As I sat down and pondered my life philosophy, I began to look back throughout my life and examined what has made me happy in the past. At times, when I am stressed out, I look back and see myself sitting around talking with my family or being with my girlfriend. As I look back, what gives meaning to my life is my family and friends and being there for one another. When I was a junior in college, my best friend from high school was in an accident and spent a couple of weeks in intensive care before he passed away. When something tragic happens, it makes you look at how you are living your life. What sets you apart from others? How you have been treating others? Where do you want to go? How much time do you have left to achieve your goals? Who do you want there, standing at the finish line, supporting you as you accomplish a major task? When I sit down and think about my life philosophy, that is what I think gives meaning to my life. As I took the Selective Theory Sorter, it really helped me put things into perspective. The questions are not questions that an individual would think about on a day-to-day basis. When answering the questions, I needed to sit down and think about them. My results stated that I believed thoughts lead to actions and misconceptions lead to problems. I see that a lot with the clients with whom I currently work. When a client that I am working with has a misconception, she will continue to have that misconception until she thinks about it in a different way. I also did the values exercise from Chapter 3. From this, I found I would like more peace, balance, serenity, and quality time with others. It is hard to be free from stress and emotion while going to graduate school, working 30 to 35 hours per week, finding time to do homework and study, and yet spending time with the people I love. Being able to spend time with my family and friends means a lot to me. My family has always supported me, and spending time with my family helps me achieve more balance and serenity. The results also indicated that in myself I value motivation, feeling supported, being driven, perseverance, accomplishment, balance, and even temper.

Examining my values and life philosophy helped me put things into perspective. I started thinking back a couple years about how I would never leave any time throughout my day to sit down and watch a half-hour television program or read a magazine without feeling guilty about wasting some time. I have learned to slow down and take a half-hour break or call up an old friend or a family member. I feel better when I am doing things that are important to me because they give more meaning to my life. Understanding the world around us is a necessity as we look at our life philosophy, especially because mental health counselors are working with individuals on a day-to-day basis. How a person thinks largely determines how she feels and behaves. I also think it is important to see what gives meaning to a client's life and what motivates him.

The next step is examining the schools of thought. I think I have a pretty good grasp on the schools of thought from my academic program. As I review the six schools of thought, the most appealing to me are the behavioral and pragmatic approaches. I feel that psychodynamic does not fit my thoughts or beliefs. I think I would have a hard time having a psychodynamic approach in my counseling, mostly because I do not believe in a lot of the psychoanalytic views. Behavioral theory is appealing to me because I feel that humans are shaped and determined by sociocultural conditioning and learn through conditioning and reinforcement. I also like cognitive-behavioral theory because I believe that a change in an individual's cognition will result in changes in her behaviors and actions.

I felt that taking the Selective Theory Sorter would be most beneficial to picking my own theory because it would help me determine how I view the theories. My results showed that I lean greatly toward the pragmatic school of thought, having values consistent with cognitive-behavioral therapy (CBT), rational emotive behavioral therapy (REBT), and reality therapy. They all require examining cognitions as well as client wants and needs. The three statements that I most strongly believed in were: (1) How a person thinks largely determines how that person feels and behaves, (2) irrational beliefs are the principal cause of emotional disturbance, and (3) recognizing cognitive processing in emotion and behavior is central in therapy. These results were extremely helpful in putting my views into a theoretical orientation.

As I narrowed down my schools of thought and specific theories of interest, I thought about goals and techniques I would use. I will ultimately choose goals and techniques based on my theoretical orientation. I think finding the different techniques will be easy to explore now that I have a general idea of what theoretical orientation fits my values and beliefs.

As I read the first two chapters of this text and explored the ITS model, I felt more confident in my theoretical orientation. I feel that the ITS model is beneficial for tying up the loose ends from my theories class. To understand which theory I liked best and which one would fit my values and beliefs as I counsel, the ITS model helped guide me in the right direction. I think taking the time and effort to understand and walk through the steps of the model is very beneficial. The starting point really needs to be life philosophy, how you view yourself, others around you, and the world. If your theoretical orientation does not fit your views, then it is not going to work for you or your client. I think having the life philosophy as the first step is a good choice. I like how the ITS model breaks down the school of thought and keeps it separate from the individual theories. It helped me to go through and look at the six different schools of thought before I took a look at all of the individual theories. It was not as overwhelming. Also, the techniques and goals are a good feature to have at the end of the ITS model. If you picked only your theory but did not research the techniques and goals to go with it, you would have only a theory but no way to guide your client. The ITS model helps you figure out your theoretical orientation in an easy and accurate way.

REFLECTION QUESTIONS

After reading Garrett's experience, answer the following questions:

1. What did you learn from Garrett's process?
2. What were the key moments in Garrett's learning?
3. What were the major transitions in Garrett's development as a professional helper?
4. What were your thoughts and feelings as you read Garrett's journey?
5. Which aspects of Garrett's development are similar to and/or different from your own?

Case Four: Lillian

Life Philosophy. I came back to school later in life compared to most of my classmates. I had some experiences in life that really affected me, but I did not necessarily acknowledge those before coming back to school. In my counseling theories class,

I was asked to look at my values and life philosophy. It was a very hard exercise because I was in such change. I was going through a divorce and my view of the world was altering day by day. I, actually, to be very honest, was rather bitter and angry. I had spent almost 20 years raising children, working part-time, and keeping a household together. I was a very hard worker, but I knew little about taking care of myself. I took care of everyone else. I was pretty sure that I had done no wrong and was not to blame for my martial problems. So when I went to therapy to help deal with depression and grief, I was not pleased to learn, at first, that I was part of the problem! All of this was happening while I was starting school, as I thought, to redeem myself for years of (again, as I thought) being a victim of a bad marriage.

In my theories class I was asked to look at myself. Me—not others around me—but to look truly at me. It was hard. Very hard. I actually was mad at the professor at first. I did not like the assignment. But as I looked at myself and I was going to therapy, I learned that I was part of the problem of what was going on in my life. I wasn't really happy to learn that! But it helped me because I think today I am a better counselor for it.

What I learned in class supported my learning in therapy. I had spent a lot of years being the "woman" at home, and when my children were moving out of the house, my role changed. And my husband at the time and I did not know what else I had to offer. It was such a hard time because my foundation of who I was gone. But it also, looking back, was an exciting time because I was able really to grow and become something new,

School of Thought. I was asked to look at my school of thought in my class. This was hard because I was really inspired by the family theories and feminism. I was worried I liked feminism simply because I was mad at my ex-husband. I learned this was not true, however. Feminism made sense to me because I saw I was placed (and put myself) in a traditionally feminine role and that when that role became obsolete in my family, with my children growing up, I was lost.

I also learned at this time about the family theories. These really made sense to me. I had really thought, before my counseling theories course and therapy, I was what was "wrong" in my marriage. I was learning, and still am, that my role in my marriage, and my family, was part of a bigger picture. I really liked learning about the family theories. They made such sense to me because I was learning the role I played in my problems but also learning I was just part of the problem. It was important for me to learn that I was not the cause of others' unhappiness. It may seem like common sense to others, but it was a revelation to me!

Theory. The family theories and feminism seemed so fitting to me when I was asked to pick a theory. It was hard to decide. However, I thought feminism was something I could put into whatever counseling theory I chose. I untimely looked at my own beliefs and came to realize that within the family theories, I really believed that values and beliefs are passed down from previous generations. I saw that the role I played in my immediate family was similar to the roles my mother, grandmother, and, as I learned in class, my great-grandmother, played. So Bowen family therapy made great sense to me. I also learned that the role I tried to play for so long was similar to the role women played in my ex-husband's family. But when I changed, he, our family, and I were not really ready. And we did not, as a family, change with me.

Goals and Techniques. It was clear to me, that the family theories made sense for me, at least when I applied them to me. I was really relieved to see that, once I started seeing clients, the family theories made sense there as well. I was able to work successfully with my clients from a family therapy perspective and help them. I loved that it worked so well for my clients and me! I feel like I have healed, and I see my clients heal as well.

I am just beginning to work as a counselor, so I am still working on what goals and techniques I should use. I do know that my clients, like I did, sure learn a lot about themselves and their families from doing genograms and gaining insight. I have clients come in who think their concerns have nothing to do with their family, yet they learn so much from looking at their immediate family and their family of origin.

I am so pleased I found an approach that works for me both personally and professionally. I find that as a counselor I am able to be congruent with who I am and what I do professionally. I have learned so much about being a competent counselor but also how to be a compassionate counselor. Having a theoretical orientation that matches my personal beliefs has helped me to be confident and effective in my counseling.

REFLECTION QUESTIONS

After reading Lillian's experience, answer the following questions:

1. Why do you suppose Lillian chose a family therapy instead of feminist therapy as a working theoretical orientation?
2. What would you focus on if Lillian were your client in a client-counselor relationship?
3. How do you see the role of person and counselor interacting as you learn about Lillian?
4. What were your thoughts and feelings as you read Lillian's experience?
5. Are there parts of Lillian's experience to which you could relate?

Comment on the Cases

Each of the helpers described their experiences working through the ITS model and striving to find their theoretical orientation. Because each of them approached the ITS model in a different way, with unique experiences and personalities, each had unique results. Evan's experience reflects that of a new helping professional who has struggled a great deal with his own emotional growth during his educational process of becoming a helping professional, which is a common experience for many counselors. Jill's experience reflects a person confident in her theoretical orientation and ways of viewing the world. Lillian's and Garrett's experiences, through divorce and family changes and the death of someone close, respectively, both ended with a clear understanding of themselves and with clearer priorities.

Now that you have had a chance to see how other helpers have used the ITS model, you will have the opportunity to read about ways the model can be used in both clinical and supervision situations. The model is valuable not only in determining your own theoretical orientation but also in helping you to work effectively with clients.

CLIENT CASE STUDIES

These clinical cases are representative of clients you may see in your work as a helping professional. After each case is presented, you will have the opportunity to respond to the reflection questions that follow.

Case One: Tony

Tony is a 28-year-old, African American male who lives alone and attends graduate school on a part-time basis. He supports himself by working as a stock clerk in a local department store. He completed his coursework for a master's degree in human resources four years ago, but he has yet to begin the thesis needed to earn the degree. Tony presents with flat affect and reports being unhappy most of his life. He reports that his father had a history of drug use and that his mother died of a cocaine overdose when he was 12 years old. Tony reports no history of drug or alcohol use. He is seeking counseling to deal with his relationships with women. His current relationship is the longest he has ever sustained. He states that girlfriends find him "too clingy," and it appears that his current girlfriend of eight months is also frustrated by his neediness. Tony wants to make this relationship work. He feels that his girlfriend is "the one" and wants your help learning new ways to be "less clingy."

REFLECTION QUESTIONS

1. What concerns do you have about working with Tony?
2. How does your life philosophy affect your view of Tony?
3. Which of your personal values might affect your work with Tony?
4. What, if any, cultural factors might play a role in your relationship with Tony?
5. Which theory or theories parallel your values and views?
6. What goals will you set and what techniques will you use in your work with Tony?

Case Two: Nancy

Nancy is a 38-year-old Vietnamese woman seeking treatment to determine "what to do about my marriage." Nancy reports that her husband is "nice but annoys me." Nancy states that she has stayed in her marriage because people would think she "is an idiot to leave a guy as great as her husband." Nancy states that both she and her husband were "boat people" who immigrated to the United States as children. Nancy's parents were pleased that she married "another Vietnamese," especially because the families have been friends for several generations. Nancy has been married for 13 years and has engaged in "a couple of other relationships" since the second year of her marriage. Nancy states that one of her extramarital relationships has gone on for 11 years. She believes this extramarital relationship is "exactly what" she really wants. However, she feels stuck. Nancy wants your help making this "huge" decision about her marriage.

REFLECTION QUESTIONS

1. How does your life philosophy affect your view of Nancy?
2. Which of your personal values might affect your work with Nancy?
3. What, if any, cultural factors might play a role in your relationship with Nancy?
4. Which theory or theories parallel your values and views?
5. What goals will you set and what techniques will you use in your work with Nancy?

Case Three: Brenda

Brenda is a 19-year-old, Caucasian college sophomore. She is seeking counseling to deal with three issues: (1) her feelings of depression, (2) her tendencies toward perfectionism, and (3) her fear of feeling attracted to women. In your work with Brenda, she determines that she needs medication for her depression. A doctor at the student health clinic gives her a prescription, and she feels "a lot less depressed" within a month of beginning the medication. Brenda continues coming to see you. In your work together, she realizes that her depression and perfectionism are due to her "romantic feelings toward women." Brenda decides that she would like to focus her time with you on figuring out whether she is a lesbian. Specifically, she wants help figuring out how her feelings toward people of the same gender intersect with her Christian upbringing. Brenda is also concerned about how her family members and friends may react to her *if* she is a lesbian.

REFLECTION QUESTIONS

1. What positive and negative biases do you bring to your work with Brenda?
2. How does your life philosophy affect your view of Brenda?
3. How might your personal and/or spiritual values affect your work with Brenda?
4. What, if any, cultural factors might play a role in your relationship with Brenda?
5. Which theory or theories parallel your values and views?
6. What goals will you set and what techniques will you use in your work with Brenda?

SUPERVISION CASE STUDIES

You have experienced the ITS model as a tool with which to examine theoretical orientation as well as some clinical cases. Now, you will have the opportunity to use the model in a supervision setting. Many clinicians in the helping professions have rather strong opinions regarding clinical supervision. Specifically, you may be familiar with the supervisory styles you like and do not like. You may be able to recall certain interventions and strategies that worked better for you than others. As a professional helper, you too will likely have the opportunity to serve as a clinical supervisor because professional helpers are often asked or required to supervise students and colleagues new to the profession. In your role as a supervisor, you may find the ITS model helpful to you. The following cases offer the chance to apply the model with those whom you will supervise.

Case One: Grace

As a seasoned mental health counselor who works in a community agency, you have been asked to supervise a new mental health counselor named Grace. In your weekly supervision meetings, you notice how easily Grace engages you. She is very affective-oriented. Her level of empathy and reflection of feeling are far greater than you would anticipate from someone with this level of experience. You perceive that Grace is humanistic-oriented. Unfortunately, you are surprised when you watch the video recordings of her counseling sessions. In every session, she tries to do behavior modification. She approaches nearly each session, regardless of the client's issue, with a preset plan for behavior modification. You notice that Grace is so intent on behavior modification that she misses what the clients are saying.

REFLECTION QUESTIONS

Using the ITS model as a guide, answer the following questions:

1. How can you help Grace pick a theory that is more congruent with who she is as a person?
2. How would your own theoretical orientation hinder or help your work with Grace?
3. Where do you think Grace falls on the ITS model of making theory practical?

Case Two: Casey

You are the director of a college counseling center and have taken on the supervision of a new, master's-level intern named Casey. He is eager to work with college students and believes he is an existentialist and "really open to feedback." In your supervision of Casey, you are consistently impressed with his ability to build rapport with clients and construct meaning in their stories. He is caring and open to concerns that clients share with him. He tells you during a supervision meeting that he "really likes" one of his clients because of the growth she is attempting. When you watch the video recording, you notice that Casey seems to be flirting with the client rather than conducting therapy. You ask Casey about his nonverbal communication with the client, and he states that he is "just concerned" about her. As you watched more of the recording, you noticed that Casey barely utilizes any counseling skills. When you confront Casey about your concerns, he says, "You must not have watched the whole recording!" He is enraged and unable to hear your concerns about his potential attraction to the client.

REFLECTION QUESTIONS

Using the ITS model as a guide, answer the following questions:

1. How can you help Casey achieve more congruence between his stated theoretical orientation and his recorded behavior?

2. How can you help Casey use his existential theory to understand what you see as countertransference?

3. How would your own theoretical orientation hinder or help your work with Casey?

4. Which pieces of the ITS model of making theory practical would be most relevant for Casey to revisit?

Case Three: Dominic

You are the director for your city's hospice program, which serves clients battling different types of illness, and you are supervising Dominic, a staff counselor with 10 years of experience. Dominic has worked at the hospice facility for three years and has received excellent evaluations each year. Lately, you have heard from Dominic's clients that he seems less interested than he once did. Many clients have complained that Dominic wants them to go to group therapy instead of seeing him so frequently as individual counseling clients. In your concern for Dominic and the clients, you talk with him. During the course of the conversation, Dominic shares with you that his way of looking at the world has changed. His wife is battling cancer, and Dominic reports that they have greatly benefited from group therapy. He thinks group therapy is underutilized among people and families with cancer. He would like you to expand his position so that he can provide both individual and group counseling. You want to be sensitive to Dominic as a colleague and friend. However, his job requires that he provide individual counseling to the clients served by your office. Group counseling is provided under contract by another agency.

REFLECTION QUESTIONS

Using the ITS model as a guide, answer the following questions:

1. Which steps of the ITS model would you recommend Dominic examine?

2. How can you help Dominic to incorporate his values into his work?

3. What recommendations would you make to Dominic to ensure that he has sufficient support?

Summary of Supervision Case Studies

The ITS model can serve as both a practical and a conceptual tool in the helping professions. In this chapter, we have presented numerous ways in which the model can be applied by students, professional helpers, and supervisors. In finding your theoretical orientation, you may have challenges along the way, which was made clear in several of the case studies. When working with specific client populations, your specific theory and values may be challenged because many clients will have a worldview that diverges from your own. As a future supervisor, you may also find yourself wanting to assist helpers as they develop and solidify their theoretical orientation.

Choosing a theory that is based on your personal life philosophy and values has an extra challenge because life experiences will change your worldview. As shown in the case examples, transitions will likely challenge you in personal and professional endeavors. Life philosophy is the foundation of the ITS model. As a developing professional, you may find that intermittently reviewing your own theoretical development is necessary and refreshing.

PUTTING IT ALL TOGETHER

Importance Revisited

Theoretical orientations in the helping professions serve many purposes. Accountability and intentionality are important aspects to the field of counseling because actions and words may have huge impacts on the lives of clients. Research has driven the effectiveness of counseling theory; consequently, helpers must provide techniques and interventions that have been proven to work. The only way helpers can do this is to be founded in theory. Legal mandates, ethical codes, and informed consent also require that helping professionals have a personal theoretical orientation and be able to articulate it.

Having a defined theory is important to the work of a counselor because theory can serve as a road map to understanding the direction to take with clients. When counselors need direction both during and outside the therapy session, theory can serve as a conceptual tool to aid them.

How Theory Is Found

Training programs often require students to articulate their theory of counseling. However, students are often given little support in choosing a theory from which to work. Most students find their theory in one of four ways: (1) They choose the theoretical orientation of the helper's training program, (2) they rely on the helper's life philosophy, (3) they rely on the helper's experience as a helper and/or a client (Hackney, 1992), or (4) they embrace research-driven approaches (Halbur & Halbur, 2011). However, each of these traditional methods has its unique weaknesses.

The ITS model was developed to meet the need for a more comprehensive model for choosing a theory. The model offers direction in finding a theory of counseling and in finding a theory that is congruent with one's life philosophy and values. It is based on life philosophy. Through processes such as value clarification or the Selective Theory Sorter–Revised (STS–R), counselors may explore their own beliefs and values. This exploration is the first step in finding a theoretical orientation that is congruent with core beliefs. Once counselors achieve this difficult objective of identifying their life philosophy, they can look at the already existing body of knowledge to see what school of thought and theory best fit them. Luckily, research on effective therapies already exists, and counselors can pursue and digest the material already available.

Benefit of the ITS Model to the Field

The ITS model can serve several purposes. First, it provides direction for students and clinicians seeking their theories. For some, it is a good first step for beginning or continuing the important process of choosing and solidifying a comprehensive theoretical orientation. As life experiences and transitions occur, however, professionals and clinicians in the field may seek to again hone or change their theoretical orientation. The foundation of the ITS model is rooted in self-reflection and identifying one's life philosophy. This challenge, addressed within these pages, is a meaningful endeavor; however, it is an ongoing endeavor. Life experiences affect counselors just as they do our clients. Therefore, it is important that counselors be amenable to the fluidity of life as it changes one's life philosophy and possibly changes one's theoretical orientation. These experiences and changes ultimately affect clients.

For educators, supervisors, and researchers, the ITS serves as a conceptual clinical tool outside the therapy hour. It helps us to view the development of counselors as they choose their theoretical orientation of counseling. Being anchored in theory, as mentioned throughout this text, is fundamental in providing ethical, intentional, and effective therapy (Halbur & Halbur, 2011). Choosing a theoretical orientation is a vital part of most clinicians' development, and the ITS model provides a framework for understanding this development and being intentional in this process.

The primary goal of the ITS model is to reach those professionals and students facing theoretical challenges. Having a theoretical orientation is a core component of being a counselor, even though the various theoretical orientations have similar efficacy (Halbur & Halbur, 2011; Wampold, 2001) when applied clinically. Finding a theoretical orientation is often a daunting task for many clinicians (Halbur & Halbur, 2006). What is important is that the theoretical orientation of counselors is congruent with who they are and their life philosophy, and helps them to serve clients ethical, competently and in an enjoyable way. The ITS model may assist neophyte as well as seasoned counselors in this process.

The helping professions are dynamic and evolving. Counselors, social workers, and psychologists all have careers that serve the public in important ways. Through prevention and therapy, these meaningful fields provide unique opportunities for both the public and the profession. Professionals in the helping fields are constantly challenging the clients they serve; however, these professionals must also accept being continuously challenged. Clients are constantly asked to seek, grow, and change. Counselors have this same opportunity to change, both as professionals and as people.

References

Adler, A., Ansbacher, H. L., & Ansbacher, R. R. (1989). *Individual psychology of Alfred Adler: A systematic presentation in selections from his writings.* New York, NY: HarperCollins.

Ansbacher, H. L. (1985). The significance of Alfred Adler for the concept of narcissism. *American Journal of Psychiatry, 142,* 203–207.

Archiniega, G. M., & Newlon, B. J. (1999). Counseling and psychotherapy: Multicultural considerations. In D. Capuzzi & D. F. Gross (Eds). *Counseling and psychotherapy: Theories and interventions* (2nd ed., pp. 435–458). Upper Saddle River, NJ: Pearson.

Arthur, A. R. (2001). Personality, epistemology and psychotherapists' choice of theoretical model: A review and analysis. *European Journal of Psychotherapy, Counseling, and Health, 4,* 45–64.

Assay, T. P., & Lambert, M. J. (1999). The empirical case for the common factors in therapy: Quantitative findings. In M. A. Hubble, B. L. Duncan, & S. D. Miller (Eds.), *The heart and soul of change: What works in therapy* (pp. 33–56). Washington, DC: American Psychological Association.

Bandura, A. (1969). *Principles of behavior modification.* New York, NY: Holt, Rinehart & Winston.

Beck, A. T. (1976). *Cognitive therapy and the emotional disorders.* New York, NY: International Universities Press.

Beck, A. T. (1991). Cognitive therapy: A 30-year retrospective. *American Psychologist, 46,* 368–375.

Becker, D. (2006). Therapy for the middle-aged: The relevance of existential issues. *American Journal of Psychotherapy, 60*(1), 87–99.

Berg, K. B. (2003). *Children's solution work.* New York, NY: W. W. Norton.

Bohart, A. C., O'Hara, M., & Leitner, L. M. (1998). Empirically violated treatments: Disenfranchisement of humanistic and other psychotherapies. *Psychotherapy Research, 8,* 141–157.

Bowen, M. (1966). The use of family theory in clinical practice. *Comprehensive Psychiatry 7,* 345–374.

Brown, L. S., & Bryan, T. C. (2007). Feminist therapy with people who self-inflict violence. *Journal of Clinical Psychology, 63*(11), 1121–1133.

Burnwell, R., & Chen, C. P. (2002). Applying REBT to workaholic clients. *Counseling Psychology Quarterly, 15*(3), 219–228.

Cashin, A. (2008). Narrative therapy: A psychotherapeutic approach in the treatment of adolescents with Asperger's disorder. *Journal of Child and Adolescent Psychiatric Nursing, 21*(1), 48–56.

Chamless D. L., et al. (1998). An update on empirically validated therapies, II. *The Clinical Psychologist 51*(1), 3–15.

Corey, G. (2004). *Theory and practice of counseling and psychotherapy* (5th ed.). Pacific Grove, CA: Wadsworth.

Corey, G. (2012). *Theory and practice of counseling and psychotherapy* (9th ed.). Pacific Grove, CA: Cengage.

Corsini, R. J. (1979). *Current psychotherapies* (2nd ed.). Itasca, IL: F. E. Peacock.

Craske, M. C., & Zunker, B. G. (2001). Consideration of the APA practice guideline for the treatment of patients with panic disorder: Strengths and limitations for behavior therapy. *Behavior Therapy 32,* 259–281.

Daly, B. P., Creed, T., Xanthopoulos, M., & Brown, R. T. (2007). Psychosocial treatments for children with attention deficit/hyperactivity disorder. *Neuropsychological Review, 17,* 73–89.

Day, S. X. (2004). *Theory and design in counseling and psychotherapy.* Boston, MA: Houghton Mifflin.

de Shazer, S. (1985). *Keys to solution in brief therapy.* New York, NY: W. W. Norton.

Dinkmeyer, D. (2007). A systemic approach to marriage education. *Journal of Individual Psychology, 63*(3), 315–321.

Doyle, R. E. (1998). *Essential skills and strategies in the helping process*. Pacific Grove, CA: Brooks/Cole.

Drapela, V. J. (1990). The value of theories for counseling. *International Journal for the Advancement of Counseling 13*, 19–26.

Duncan, B. L. (2002). The legacy of Saul Rosenzweig: The profundity of the dodo bird. *Journal of Psychotherapy Integration, 12*, 32–57.

Ellis, A. (1962). *A reason and emotion in psychotherapy*. New York, NY: Lyle Stuart.

Enns, C. Z. (1993). Twenty years of feminist counseling and therapy: From naming biases to implementing multifaceted practice. *Counseling Psychologist, 21*(1), 3–87.

Erford, B. T., Eaves, S. H., Bryant, E. M., & Young, K. A. (2010). *35 techniques every counselor should know*. Upper Saddle River, NJ: Pearson.

Erickson, D. B. (1993). The relationship between personality type and preferred counseling model. *Journal of Psychological Type, 27*, 39–41.

Figley, C. R., & Nelson, T. S. (1990). Basic family therapy skill, II: Structural family therapy. *Journal of Marital and Family Therapy, 16*(3), 225–239.

Frank, J. (1973). *Persuasion and healing: A comparative study of psychotherapy* (2nd ed.). Baltimore, MD: Johns Hopkins University Press.

Frankl, V. E. (1967). *Psychotherapy and existentialism: Selected papers on Logotherapy*. New York, NY: Washington Square Press.

Frankl, V. E. (1973). *The doctor and the soul: From psychotherapy to Logotherapy* (R. Winston & C. Winston, Trans.). New York, NY: Vintage Books. (Original work published 1946 as *Ärztliche Seelsorge*)

Gerson, R., McGoldrick, M., & Petry, S. (2008). *Genograms: Assessment and intervention* (3rd ed.). New York, NY: W. W. Norton.

Gilliland, B. E., & James, R. K. (1998). *Theories and strategies in counseling and psychotherapy*. Boston, MA: Pearson.

Glasser, W. (1965). *Reality therapy: A new approach to psychiatry*. New York, NY: Guilford Press.

Glasser, W. (1998). *Choice theory: A new psychology of personal freedom*. New York, NY: HarperPerennial.

Goldenberg, H., & Goldenberg, I. (2008). *Family therapy: An overview* (7th ed.). Belmont, CA: Thomson Brooks/Cole.

Green, E. (2008). Reenvisioning Jungian analytical play therapy with child sexual assault survivors. *International Journal of Play Therapy, 2*, 102–121.

Greenberg, L. S., & Malcolm, W. (2002). Resolving unfinished business: Relating process to outcome. *Journal of Counseling and Clinical Psychology, 70*(2), 406–416.

Grencavage, L. M., & Norcross, J. C. (1990) Where are the commonalities among the therapeutic common factors? *Professional Psychology: Research and Practice 21*(5), 372–378.

Hackney, H. (1992). Differentiating between counseling theory and process. (*ERIC Digest*, ED347485)

Halbur, D. A. (2000). *A Q-methodological study of group members' experience of existential aspects of a training group*. (Unpublished doctoral dissertation). University of South Dakota, Vermillion.

Halbur, D. A., & Halbur, K. V. (2006). *Developing your theoretical orientation in counseling and psychotherapy*. Boston, MA: Pearson.

Halbur, D. A., & Halbur, K. V. (2011). *Developing your theoretical orientation in counseling and psychotherapy* (2nd ed.). Boston, MA: Pearson Education.

Haley, J. (1991). *Problem-solving therapy* (2nd ed.). New York, NY: Jossey-Bass.

Hansen, J. C., Rossberg, R. K., & Cramer, S. H. (1993). *Counseling: Theory and process* (5th ed.). Boston, MA: Pearson.

Hansen, N. E., & Freimuth, M. (1997). Piecing the puzzle together: A model for understanding the theory-practice relationship. *Counseling Psychologist, 25*(4), 654–673.

Hazler, R. J. (2003). Person-centered theory. In D. Capuzzi & D. R. Gross (Eds.), *Counseling and psychotherapy: Theories and interventions* (3rd ed., pp. 157–180). Upper Saddle River, NJ: Pearson.

Hoffman, P. D., & Steiner-Grossman, P. (2012). *Borderline personality disorder: Meeting the challenges to successful treatment*. New York, NY: Routledge.

Ivey, A. E., D'Andrea, M., Ivey, M. B., & Simek-Morgan, L. (2002). *Theories of counseling and psychotherapy: A multicultural perspective.* Boston, MA: Pearson.

Ivey, A. E., & Ivey, M. B. (1999). *Intentional interviewing and counseling: Facilitating client development in a multicultural society.* Pacific Grove, CA: Wadsworth.

Ivey, A. E., Ivey, M. B., D'Andrea, M., & Simek-Morgan, L. (2007). *Counseling and psychotherapy: A multicultural perspective* (6th ed.). Boston, MA: Pearson.

Ivey, A. E., Ivey, M. B., & Simek-Downing, L. (1987). *Counseling and psychotherapy: Integrating skills, theory, and practice.* Englewood Cliffs, NJ: Pearson.

Ivey, A. E., Ivey, M. B., & Simek-Morgan, L. (1997). *Counseling and psychotherapy: A multicultural perspective* (4th ed.). Boston, MA: Pearson.

Jackson, M., & Thompson, C. L. (1971). Effective counselors: Characteristics and attitudes. *Journal of Counseling Psychology, 18*(3), 249–254.

Johnson, R., & Halbur, D. A. (2013). Strength of theoretical orientation among first year counseling students. *NC Perspectives, 8*(1), 42–51.

Jongsma, A. E., & Peterson, L. M. (1995). *The complete adult psychotherapy treatment planner.* New York, NY: John Wiley.

Jung, C. G. (1991). *The development of personality: Papers on child psychology, education and related subjects* (5th ed.) (H. Head, M. Fordham, G. Ader, & W. McGuire, Eds., R. F. C. Hull, Trans.). New York, NY: Princeton University Press.

Kaufman, Y. (1979). Analytical psychotherapy. In R. J. Corsini (Ed.), *Current psychotherapies* (pp. 95–130). Itasca, IL: F. E. Peacock.

Klein, M. (1975). *Envy and gratitude and other works.* London, England: Hogarth Press.

Kottler, J. A. (1999). *The nuts and bolts of helping.* Boston, MA: Pearson.

Kottler, J. A., & Brown, R. W. (1992). *Introduction to therapeutic counseling* (2nd ed.). Pacific Grove, CA: Peacock.

Lantz, J. (1989). Family Logotherapy with an overweight family. *Contemporary Family Therapy, 11*(4), 287–297.

Lazarus A. A. (1989). *The practice of multimodal therapy: Systematic, comprehensive, and effective psychotherapy.* Baltimore, MD: Johns Hopkins University Press.

Leibert, T. W. (2011). The dimensions of common factors in counseling. *International Journal of Advanced Counseling 33,* 127–138.

Li, L. C., Kim, B. S., & O'Brien, K. M. (2007). An analogue study of the effects of Asian cultural values and counselor multicultural competence on counseling process. *Psychotherapy Theory, Research, Practice, Training, 44*(1), 90–95.

Lloyd, H., & Dallos, R. (2006). Solution-focused brief therapy with families who have a child with intellectual disabilities: A description of the content of initial sessions and processes. *Clinical Child Psychology and Psychiatry, 11*(3), 367–386.

Luborsky, L., Singer, B., & Luborsky, L. (1975). Comparative studies of psychotherapies: Is it true that "everyone has won and all must have prizes"? *Archives of General Psychiatry, 32,* 995–1008.

Madanes, C. (1981). *Strategic family therapy.* New York, NY: Jossey-Bass.

Mahoney, M. (1991). *Human change processes: The scientific foundations of psychotherapy.* New York, NY: Basic Books.

Mancoske, R. J., Standifer, D., & Cauley, C. (1994). The effectiveness of brief counseling services for battered women. *Research on Social Work Practice, 4*(1), 53–56.

Maniacci, M. (2007). His majesty the baby: Narcissism through the lens of individual psychology. *Journal of Individual Psychology, 63*(2), 136–145.

Matsuyuki, M. (1998). Japanese feminist counseling as a political act. *Women and Therapy, 21*(2), 65–77.

May, R. (1983). *Existential psychology.* New York, NY: Random House.

McClary, R. (2007). Healing the psyche through music, myth, and ritual. *Psychology of Aesthetics, Creativity, and the Arts, 1*(3), 155–159.

McCloskey, M. S., Noblett, K. L., Deffenbacher, J. L., Gollan, J. K., & Coccaro, E. F. (2008). Cognitive-behavioral therapy for intermittent explosive disorder: A pilot randomized clinical trial. *Journal of Counseling and Clinical Psychology, 76*(5), 876–886.

Minuchin, S. (1974). *Families and family therapy.* Cambridge, MA: Harvard University Press.

Mosak, H. H. (1979). Adlerian psychotherapy. In R. J. Corsini (Ed.), *Current psychotherapy* (2nd ed., pp. 44–94). Itasca, IL: Peacock.

Mosak, H. H. (1985). Interrupting a depression: The pushbutton technique. *Journal of Individual Psychology, 41*, 210–214.

Murdock, N. (2009). *Theories of counseling and psychotherapy: A case approach* (2nd ed.). Columbus, OH: Pearson.

Murdock, N. (2012). *Theories of counseling and psychotherapy: A case approach* (3rd ed.). Columbus, OH: Pearson.

Myers, I. B., & McCaulley, M. H. (1985). *Manual: A guide to the development and use of the Myers-Briggs Type Indicator.* Palo Alto, CA: Consulting Psychologists Press.

Myers, I. B., & McCaulley, M. H. (1998). *Manual: A guide to the development and use of the Myers-Briggs Type Indicator.* Palo Alto, CA: Consulting Psychologists Press.

Myers, I. B., & Myers, K. D. (1977). *Myers-Briggs Type Indicator, Form G.* Palo Alto, CA: Consulting Psychologists Press.

Myers, K. (1993). Isabel Briggs Myers and type development. *Bulletin of Psychological Type, 16*(4), 6–8.

Nelson-Jones, R. (2000). *Six key approaches to counseling and therapy.* New York, NY: Continuum.

Nichols, M. P. (2008). *Family therapy: Concepts and methods* (8th ed.). Boston, MA: Pearson Education.

Nichols, M. P., & Schwartz, R. C. (2001). *Family therapy: Concept and methods* (5th ed.). Boston, MA: Pearson.

Norcross, J. C. (1997). Emerging breakthroughs in psychotherapy integration: Three predictions and one fantasy. *Psychotherapy, 34*(1), 86–90.

Norcross, J. C. (2005). A primer on psychotherapy integration. In J. C. Norcross & M. R. Goldfried (Eds.), *Handbook of psychotherapy integration* (2nd ed.). New York, NY: Oxford University Press.

Pagoto, S., Bodenlos, J. S., Schneider, K. L., Olendzki, B., & Spates, C. R. (2008). Initial investigation of behavioral activation therapy for co-morbid major depressive disorder and obesity. *Psychotherapy Theory, Research, Practice, Training, 45*(3), 410–415.

Parsons, R. D. (2009). *Translating theory to practice: Thinking and acting like an expert counselor.* Upper Saddle River, NJ. Pearson.

Pedersen, P. B., Draguns, J. G., Lonner, W. J., & Trimble, J. E. (Eds.). (1996). *Counseling across cultures.* Thousand Oaks, CA: Sage.

Pedersen, P. B., & Ivey, A. E. (1993). *Culture-centered counseling and interviewing skills: A practical guide.* Westport, CT: Praeger.

Perls, F. S. (1969a). *Gestalt therapy verbatim.* Moab, UT: Real People Press.

Perls, F. S. (1969b). *In and out of the garbage pail.* Moab, UT: Real People Press.

Poznanski, J. J., & McLennan, J. (1995). Conceptualizing and measuring counselors' theoretical orientation. *Journal of Counseling Psychology, 42*(4), 411–422.

Prenzlau, S. (2006). Using reality therapy to reduce PTSD-related symptoms. *International Journal of Reality Therapy, 25*(2), 23–29.

Prochaska, J. O., & DiClemente, C. C. (1982). Transtheoretical therapy: Toward a more integrative model of change. *Psychotherapy: Theory, Research and Practice, 19*(3), 276–288.

Quinn, A. (2008). A person-centered approach to the treatment of combat veterans with post-traumatic stress disorder. *Journal of Humanistic Psychology, 48*(4), 458–476.

Rogers, C. (1957). The necessary and sufficient conditions of therapeutic personality change. *Journal of Consulting Psychology, 21*, 95–103.

Rogers, C. (1961). *On becoming a person.* Boston, MA: Houghton-Mifflin.

Rogers, C. (1995). *On becoming a person: A therapist's view of psychotherapy.* Boston, MA: Houghton Mifflin.

Rosen, H., & Kuehlwein, K. T. (1996). *Constructing realities: Meaning-making perspectives for psychotherapists.* San Francisco, CA: Jossey-Bass.

Rosenzweig, S. (1936). Some implicit common factors in diverse methods in psychotherapy. *American Journal of Orthopsychiatry, 6*, 412–415.

Rosselló, J., Bernal, G., & Rivera-Medina, C. (2008). Individual and group CPT and IPT for Puerto Rican adolescents with depressive symptoms. *Cultural Diversity and Ethnic Minority Psychology, 14*(3), 234–245.

Russell, R. L., Van de Brock, P., Adams, S., Rosenberger, K., & Essig, T. (1993). *Structural transformation of children's autogenetic stories in therapeutic retelling: An empirical investigation.* Paper presented at the 18th conference of the Society for Psychotherapy Research, Ulm, West Germany.

Safer, D. L., Telch, C. F., Chen, E. Y., & Linhan, M. M. (2009). *Dialectical behavior therapy for binge eating and bulimia.* New York: Guilford Press.

Saltzburg, A. (2007). Narrative therapy pathways for re-authoring with parents of adolescents coming-out as lesbian, gay, and bisexual. *Contemporary Family Therapy, 29*, 57–69.

Schmidt, E. A. (2001). Dismantling eclecticism: Choosing, understanding, and implementing a legitimate theory of counseling. *TCA Journal, 29*(1), 96–103.

Sharp, S. R., & MaCallum, R. S. (2005). A rational emotive behavioral approach to improve anger management and reduce office referrals in middle school children: A formative investigation and evaluation. *Journal of Applied School Psychology, 21*(1), 39–59.

Skinner, B. F. (1971). *Beyond freedom and dignity.* New York, NY: Free Press.

Skinner, B. F. (1976). *Walden two.* Boston, MA: Pearson.

Snyder, M. (2002). Applications of Carl Rogers' theory and practice to couple and family therapy: A response to Harlen Anderson and David Bott. *Journal of Family Therapy, 24*, 317–315.

Srebalus, D., & Brown, D. (2001). *A guide to the helping professions.* Boston, MA: Pearson.

Strohmer, D. V., Shivy, V. A., & Chodo, A. L. (1990). Information processing strategies in counselor hypotheses testing: The role of selective memory and expectancy. *Journal of Counseling Psychology, 37*(4), 465–472.

Strupp, H. H. (1955). An objective comparison of Rogerian and psychoanalytic techniques. *Journal of Consulting Psychology, 19*, 1–7.

Sue, D. W., & Sue, D. (2003). *Counseling the culturally diverse: Theory and practice* (4th ed.). New York, NY: John Wiley.

Sue, D. W., & Sue, D. (2008). *Foundations of counseling and psychotherapy: Evidenced-based practices for a diverse society.* New York, NY: John Wiley.

Tomasulo, D. J., & Razza, N.J. (2009) Empirical validation of IBT for clients with intellectual disabilities. *The Group Psychologist, 19*(3), 6–8.

Wampold, B. E. (2001). *The great psychotherapy debate: Models, methods, and findings.* Mahwah, NJ: Lawrence Erlbaum.

Wampold, B. E., Mondin, G. W., Moody, M., Stich, F., Benson, K., & Ahn, H. (1997). A meta-analysis of outcome studies comparing bona fide psychotherapies: Empirically, "all must have prizes." *Psychological Bulletin, 122*, 203–215.

Watts, R. (1993). Developing a personal theory of counseling: A brief guide for students. *TCA Journal, 21*(1), 103–104.

Weiskeop, S., Richdale, A., & Matthews, J. (2005). Behavioural treatment to reduce sleep problems in children with autism or fragile X syndrome. *Developmental Medicine and Child Neurology, 47*(2), 94–104.

Weist, D. J., Wong, E. H., Brotherton, S., & Cervantes, J. M. (2001). Postmodern counseling: Using narrative approaches in the school setting. *Family Therapy, 28*(1), 1–17.

White, M. (2007). *Maps of narrative therapy.* New York, NY: W. W. Norton.

Wilde, J. (2008). Rational-emotive behavioral interventions for children with anxiety problems. *Journal of Cognitive and Behavioral Psychotherapies, 8*(1), 133–141.

Willis, C. T. (1989). The Myers-Briggs Type Indicator. In D. J. Keyser & R. C. Sweetland (Eds.), *Test critiques* (Vol. 10). Austin, TX: Pro-Ed.

Wrenn, R. L. (1960). Counselor orientation: Theoretical or situational. *Journal of Counseling Psychology*, 7(1), 40–45.

Wubbolding, R. E. (2000). *Reality therapy for the 21st century*. Philadelphia, PA: Brunner Routledge.

Yalom, I. D. (1980). *Existential psychotherapy*. New York, NY: Basic Books.

Yalom, I. D. (1995). *Group psychotherapy*. New York, NY: Basic Books.

Yalom, I. D. (2002). *Gift of therapy: An open invention to a new generation of therapists and their patients*. New York, NY: HarperPerennial.

Young, M. E. (1998). *Learning the art of helping*. Upper Saddle River, NJ: Pearson.

Zimmerman, J. L., & Dickerson, V. C. (1996). *If problems talked: Narrative therapy in action*. New York, NY: Guilford Press.

Index

Note: Information presented in tables and figures is denoted by *t* or *f* respectively.

A
ABC method, 73
Actualization, 65
Adler, Alfred, 55–58, 86
Advocacy, 81
Allegiance factor, 9
Anal stage, 50
Analytical theory
   background of, 53
   diversity and, 55
   family approaches in, 86
   goals of, 54
   life philosophy and, 53–54
   suggested readings and websites on, 41
   summary of, 46*t*
   techniques of, 54–55
Androgyny and assertiveness training, 81
Archetypal analysis, 54, 55
Archetypes, 53
Aversion therapy, 60
Avoiding-type personality, 57
Awareness, 65

B
Beck, Aaron, 70
Behavioral contracting, 3
Behavioral theory
   suggested readings and websites on, 41–42
   summary of, 46*t*
Behavioral therapy
   diversity and, 60
   explanation of, 58, 61*f*
   goals of, 60
   Intentional Theory Selection model and, 61
   life philosophy and, 59–60
   techniques of, 60
Bisexuals. *See* LGBT (lesbian, gay, bisexual, or transgender) individuals
Boundaries, 89
Boundary making, 90
Bowen, Murray, 86–88
Bowen family systems therapy
   function of, 86
   goals of, 87
   life philosophy and, 87
   suggested readings and websites on, 44
   summary of, 47*t*
   techniques of, 87–88
Briggs, Katherine, 36

C
Case studies
   client, 102–103
   clinician, 93–102
   supervision, 104–106
Castration, fear of, 50
CBT. *See* Cognitive-behavioral therapy (CBT)
Classical conditioning, 59, 60
Client case studies, 102–103
Client-centered approach. *See* Person-centered approach
Clinician case studies, 93–102
Cognitive-behavioral therapy (CBT)
   diversity and, 71–72
   function of, 8, 70
   goals of, 71
   life philosophy and, 70–71
   suggested readings and websites on, 43
   summary of, 46*t*
   techniques of, 71
Collective unconscious, 53
Conditional response, 59
Confrontation, 73
Constellation, 57
Constructivist school of thought
   background of, 76–77
   feminist therapy and, 79–81
   multicultural counseling and therapy and, 77–79
   narrative therapy and, 81–84
   solution-focused brief therapy and, 84–86
   suggested readings and websites on, 43–44
Contracts, 75
Counselors
   culturally competent, 77–78
   diversity among, 21, 24
   professional development opportunities for, 38, 39
   selection of theoretical orientation by (*See* Theoretical orientation; Theoretical orientation selection methods)
Counselors-in-training
   observation of, 23–24
   real-world experiences for, 38–39
Creative power, 56
Cultural diversity. *See* Diversity
Cultural feminists, 80, 81
Culture, 20–21. *See also* Diversity; Multicultural counseling and therapy (MCT)

D
Deconstructivists, 49
Defense mechanisms, 49, 51
Dialectical behavioral therapy (DBT), 8
Directives, 88
Disengaged, 89
Diversity
   analytical theory and, 55
   behaviorism and, 60
   cognitive-behavioral therapy and, 71–72
   existential approach and, 66
   family therapies and, 91–92
   feminist therapies and, 81
   Gestalt therapy and, 70
   individual psychology and, 58
   multicultural counseling and therapy and, 79
   narrative therapy and, 84
   nature of, 21
   person-centered approach and, 64
   psychoanalysis and, 51–52
   rational emotive behavioral therapy and, 73
   reality therapy and, 75
   solution-focused brief therapy and, 86
Dodo bird effect, 9
Dominant-type personality, 56

Dream analysis
  analytical theory and, 54–55
  in psychoanalysis, 51, 52
Dream work (Gestalt technique), 70

E
Early recollections, 57
Eclectic approach
  feedback issues and, 22
  focus on, 21, 22
  function of, 20
Eclecticism, 6–8
Ego, 49, 51, 53, 55
Electra complex, 50
Ellis, Albert, 72
Empathy, 63
Empirically supported therapies (ESTs), 8
Empirically validated therapies (EVTs), 8–9
Empowerment feminist therapy, 81
Empty-chair technique, 3, 20, 69
Enactment, 90
Enmeshed, 89
Erikson, Milton, 88
Ethics, 10–11
Ethics codes, 11
Evidence-based theory, 6
Exceptions, 85
Existential approach
  diversity and, 66
  explanation of, 64
  goals of, 65–66
  Intentional Theory Selection Model and, 66, 67f
  life philosophy and, 64–65
  suggested readings and websites on, 42
  summary of, 46t
  techniques of, 66
Expectancy factor, 9
Externalization, 83
Extroversion/Introversion (E/I) index, 36

F
Failure identity, 74
Family approaches
  background of, 86
  Bowen family systems therapy and, 86–88
  diversity and, 91–92
  strategic family therapy and, 88–89
  structural family therapy and, 89–91, 91f
  suggested readings and websites on, 44
Family mapping, 90
Family systems theory. *See* Bowen family systems therapy

Fear of castration, 50
Feminist theories
  explanation of, 79
  suggested readings and websites on, 44
  summary of, 47t
Feminist therapy
  diversity and, 81
  function of, 79
  goals of, 80
  Intentional Theory Selection Model and, 81, 82f
  life philosophy and, 79–80
  suggested readings and websites on, 44
  summary of, 47t
  techniques of, 80–81
Fictional finalism, 56
First-order changes, 88
Free association, psychoanalytic theory and, 51, 52
Freud, Sigmund
  diversity and, 51–52
  Intentional Theory Selection model and, 52, 52f
  psychoanalysis and, 48–49, 51
  psychosexual stages and, 50
  techniques used by, 51

G
Gay. *See* LGBT (lesbian, gay, bisexual, or transgender) individuals
Gemeinschaftsgefühl, 55
Gender bias, Freud and, 51–52
Genital stage, 50
Genograms, 87
Genuineness, 63
Gestalt, 67
Gestalt psychology, 67–68
Gestalt therapy
  background of, 67
  diversity and, 70
  function of, 4
  goals of, 69
  life philosophy and, 67–69
  suggested readings and websites on, 42–43
  summary of, 46t
  techniques of, 69–70
Getting-type personality, 56–57
Gilliland, B. E., 84
Glasser, William, 74
Goals. *See also* Therapy goals
  decisions regarding, 19–20
  mistaken, 56

H
Hackney, H., 4, 5
Haley, Jay, 88

Hedonism, 59
Humanistic school of thought
  existential, 64–66, 67f
  explanation of, 61
  function of, 5
  Gestalt, 67–70
  person-centered, 62–64
  suggested readings and websites on, 42–43

I
Id, 49, 51
Ideal self, 63
Identified patient, 86
Identity, 74
Individual psychology
  background of, 55
  diversity and, 58
  goals of, 57
  life philosophy and, 55–57
  suggested readings and websites on, 41
  summary of, 46t
  techniques of, 57–58
Individuation, 53, 54
Inferiority, 56
Inferiority complex, 56
Integrative approach, focus on, 21
Intentional Theory Selection (ITS) model. *See also* Case studies; *specific theories*
  behavioral therapy and, 61
  benefits of, 107
  existential approach and, 66, 67f
  explanation of, 3, 15f
  family therapy and, 90–91, 91f
  feminist therapy and, 81, 82f
  Freud and, 52, 52f
  function of, 21, 48, 2545
  reality therapy and, 75–76, 76f
  structural family therapy and, 90–91, 91f
  theory summaries and, 46–47
Interactive behavioral therapy (IBT), 8
Interpretation, in psychoanalysis, 51
ITS model. *See* Intentional Theory Selection (ITS) model

J
James, R. K., 84
Joining and accommodating technique, 90
Judging/Perceiving (J/P) index, 37
Jung, Carl, 53–55

K
Kottler, J. A., 10

L
Latency stage, 50
Lesbian. *See* LGBT (lesbian, gay,

INDEX

bisexual, or transgender) individuals
LGBT (lesbian, gay, bisexual, or transgender) individuals, 21, 52
Liberal feminists, 80
Libidinal energy, 49, 54
Life philosophy
  analytical theory and, 53–54
  behavioral therapy and, 59–60
  Bowen family systems therapy and, 87
  case studies and, 93–96, 99–100
  cognitive-behavioral therapy and, 70–71
  existential approach and, 64–65
  feminist therapy and, 79–80
  importance of, 15–16
  individual psychology and, 55–57
  multicultural counseling and therapy and, 77
  narrative therapy and, 81–82
  person-centered approach and, 62
  psychoanalytic theory and, 49
  rational emotive behavioral therapy and, 72
  reality therapy and, 74
  solution-focused brief therapy and, 84–85
  strategic family therapy and, 88
  structural family therapy and, 89
  theoretical orientation and, 16–17, 22
Life tasks, 56
Logotherapy, 86

M
McLennan, J., 3
Mental Research Institute (MRI), 88, 89
Metaphors, 84
Miracle question, 85
Mistaken goals, 56
Multicultural counseling and therapy (MCT)
  diversity and, 79
  explanation of, 20–21, 77
  goals of, 77–78
  life philosophy and, 77
  suggested readings and websites on, 43–44
  summary of, 47t
  techniques of, 78, 80
Myers, Isabel Briggs, 36
Myers-Briggs Type Indicator (MBTI), 30, 36–37

N
Narrative therapy
  diversity and, 84
  function of, 81
  goals of, 83

life philosophy and, 81–82
  suggested readings and websites on, 44
  summary of, 47t
  techniques of, 83–84
Native Americans, 78
Nondirective approach. *See* Person-centered approach
Nonjudgment nature, 63

O
Oedipus complex, 50
Operant conditioning, 59, 60
Oral stage, 50

P
Paradoxical intervention, 89
Parenting, individual psychology and, 55–56
Pavlov, Ivan, 59
Penis envy, 50
Perls, Fritz, 67–70
Permeability, 89
Personality type
  Adler and, 56–57
  identification of, 30, 36–37
Personal unconscious, 53
Person-centered approach
  diversity and, 64
  explanation of, 62
  family approaches in, 86
  goals of, 62–63
  life philosophy and, 62
  suggested readings and websites on, 42
  summary of, 46t
  techniques of, 63–64
Phallic stage, 50
Phenomenological approach, 62
Philosophy. *See* Life philosophy
Pleasure principle, 49
Positive-addicting behaviors, 75
Poznanski, J. J., 3
Pragmatic school of thought
  background of, 70
  cognitive-behavioral therapy and, 70–72
  rational emotive behavioral therapy and, 72–73
  reality therapy and, 74–76, 76f
  suggested readings and websites on, 43
Pretend techniques, 89
Principle of closure, 67
Principle of proximity, 67
Principle of similarity, 68
Private logic, 57
Professional conferences, 38
Pronouns, Gestalt therapy and, 69
Psyche, 53, 54

Psychoanalytic theory
  background of, 48
  diversity and, 51–52
  goals of, 51
  life philosophy and, 49
  psychosexual stages and, 49, 50
  summary of, 46t
  techniques of, 51
Psychodynamic school of thought
  analytical theory, 46t, 53–55
  individual psychology, 46t, 55–58
  overview of, 48
  psychoanalytic theory, 46t, 48–52
  suggested readings and websites on, 41
Psychopathology, 55
Psychosexual stages, 49, 50
Puberty, psychoanalytic theory and, 50

R
Radical feminism, 80
Rational emotive behavioral therapy (REBT)
  diversity and, 73
  function of, 4, 5
  goals of, 73
  life philosophy and, 72
  suggested readings and websites on, 43
  summary of, 47t
  techniques of, 73
Reality principle, 49
Reality therapy
  diversity and, 75
  function of, 74
  goals of, 74
  Intentional Theory Selection Model and, 75–76, 76f
  life philosophy and, 74
  suggested readings and websites on, 43
  summary of, 47t
  techniques of, 75
Real self, 63
REBT. *See* Rational emotive behavioral therapy (REBT)
Recording techniques, 37–38
Reductionism, 56
Reframing, 89, 90
Restory, 83
Rodgerian approach. *See* Person-centered approach
Rodgers, Carl, 62, 65

S
Second-order changes, 88
Selective Theory Sorter-Revised (STS-R), 3, 30–36

INDEX

Self, 53, 54, 58
Self-actualization, 62, 68–69
Self-differentiation, 87
Sensing/iNtuition (S/N) index, 36
Sexual gratification, 49
Sharing hunches technique, 69
Skinner, B. F., 58
Social learning theory, 60
Socially useful type, 57
Solution-focused brief therapy (SFBT)
  diversity and, 86
  function of, 84
  goals of, 85
  life philosophy and, 84–85
  suggested readings and websites on, 44
  summary of, 47t
  techniques of, 85–86
Stimulus, 59
Strategic family therapy
  function of, 88
  goals of, 88
  life philosophy and, 88
  suggested readings and websites on, 44
  summary of, 47t
  techniques of, 88–89
Strength assessment, 85
Structural family therapy
  function of, 89
  goals of, 90
  Intentional Theory Selection Model and, 90–91, 91f
  life philosophy and, 89
  suggested readings and websites on, 44
  summary of, 47t
  techniques of, 90
Styles of life, 56
Subsystems, 89
Superego, 49, 51
Supervision case studies, 104–106
Systemic therapies, 86

T

Techniques. *See* Therapy techniques
Teological individuals, 56
Theoretical orientation
  application of, 10
  eclecticism as, 6–8
  effectiveness and, 9–10
  empirically validated therapies and, 8–9
  ethics and, 10–11
  function of, 4–5, 106

helping skills and, 3–4
nature of, 1–3, 5–6
personal background and belief system and, 24–25
Theoretical orientation selection methods
  articulating your values as, 29–30
  broadening your experiences as, 40
  capturing yourself as, 37–38
  finding yourself as, 28
  getting inspired by others as, 38
  identifying your personality type as, 30, 36–37
  overview of, 27, 40, 106–107
  reading about theories as, 38, 41–44
  studying with master as, 39
  surveying your preferences as, 30–36
  using real-world trials as, 38–39
Theories
  application of, 13–14
  choosing your, 18–19
  counselor resistance to, 21–23
  development of, 14–15
  schools of thought that drive, 17–18
Therapy goals
  analytical theory and, 54
  behavioral therapy and, 60
  Bowen family systems therapy and, 87
  cognitive-behavioral therapy and, 71
  existential psychotherapy and, 65–66
  feminist therapy, 80
  Gestalt therapy, 69
  individual psychology and, 57
  multicultural counseling and therapy and, 77–78
  narrative therapy and, 83
  person-centered approach and, 62–63
  psychoanalytic theory and, 51
  rational emotive behavioral therapy and, 73
  reality therapy and, 74
  solution-focused brief therapy and, 85
  strategic family therapy and, 88
  structural family therapy and, 90
Therapy techniques
  analytical theory, 54–55
  behavioral therapy, 60
  Bowen family systems therapy and, 87–88

cognitive-behavioral therapy and, 71
existential approach, 66
feminist therapy, 80–81
Gestalt therapy, 69–70
goals and, 19–20
individual psychology, 57–58
multicultural counseling and therapy, 78
narrative therapy and, 83–84
person-centered approach, 63–64
psychoanalytic theory, 51
rational emotive behavioral therapy, 73
reality therapy, 75
solution-focused brief therapy and, 85–86
strategic family therapy and, 88–89
structural family therapy and, 90
Thinking/Feeling (T/F) index, 37
Token economy, 60
Training opportunities, websites for, 39
Transference, in psychoanalysis, 51
Transgender. *See* LGBT (lesbian, gay, bisexual, or transgender) individuals
Transgenerational theory. *See* Bowen family systems therapy
Triangles, 87

U

Unbalancing, 90
Unconditional positive regard, 63
Unconditional response, 59
Unconditional stimulus, 59
Unconscious
  analytical theory and, 53
  psychoanalytic theory and, 49, 51
Unfinished business, 69

V

Values, 29–30

W

Walden Two (Skinner), 58
WDEP system, 75
Websites
  on counseling theories and approaches, 41–43
  for training opportunities, 39
White, Michael, 81

Y

Yalom, I. D., 9